"*The Christian Culture Survival Gui* [...] ever walked through the doors of [...] I laughed, related, and cheered at T[...] stereotypes to the sometimes silliness done in the name of the Father, this books cover it all with a humorous grace not found in other books about the Church." —**ANDY ARGYRAKIS**, *Chicago Tribune* contributing writer

"*The Christian Culture Survival Guide* is one of the most hilarious books I have ever read! Having been in Christian culture for most of my life, I related to so many of Matthew's stories. If you feel like you're missing something in your spiritual walk, this book is for you."
—**JACI VELASQUEZ**

"Matthew Paul Turner may not have fifty hardback non-fictions to his credit, but I grew up as a pastor's kid, and marveled at how Turner is able to articulate the tiniest, silliest nuances of staunch, homebred church life. Then, I found myself laughing, shaking my head, sighing, and smiling, all because I could relate and sympathize with every circumstance spoken of as it relates to the goings-on in what we call Contemporary Christian Music. Maybe we can all find something to relate to in these pages, and then channel our sighs into kingdom-minded innovation."
—**OWEN THOMAS**, The Elms

"Witty, insightful, edgy, cynical, hopeful, faithful, disturbing, indicting, and provocative. I promise you this: You will not come away from it with a neutral response. The story of Matt's life points to how unwelcome we Christians often can be to outsiders (and other insiders for that matter). Hitting too close to home, his *Survival Guide* is likely to be black-balled by some of the more powerful within the Christian establishment. Definitely my kind of book!" —**WILL PENNER**, editor of *Youthworker Journal*

THE
CHRISTIAN
CULTURE

THE
The Misadventures of an Outsider on the Inside
CHRISTIAN CULTURE

SURVIVAL ·GUIDE·

By Matthew Paul Turner

FOREWORD BY STEPHEN BALDWIN

[RELEVANTBOOKS]
WWW.RELEVANTBOOKS.COM

Published by Relevant Books
A division of Relevant Media Group, Inc.
www.relevantbooks.com
www.relevantmediagroup.com

© 2004 by Relevant Media Group

Design: Relevant Solutions
www.relevant-solutions.com
Cover design by Mark Arnold
Interior design by Jeremy Kennedy

For information or bulk orders:
RELEVANT MEDIA GROUP, INC.
POST OFFICE BOX 951127
LAKE MARY, FL 32795
407-333-7152

For booking info:
www.matthewpaulturner.com

Library of Congress Control Number: 2004091031
International Standard Book Number: 0-9746942-0-7

04 05 06 07 11 10 9 8 7 6 5 4 3
Printed in the United States of America

Mom, This is for you. Thank you for teaching me
to laugh, listen, and survive.

This book is in memory of my grandmother, Abby King.
Mammom's captivating spirit brought so much laughter
and life to all who knew her. I hope that someday I will
grow to have a heart as big as hers.

"It is for freedom that Christ has set us free …"
—*Galatians 5:1*

FOREWORD
BY STEPHEN BALDWIN

Since I've become a Christian, I've had so many believers ask me how God is leading me to "claim Hollywood for Jesus."

That's probably a challenge that is well beyond one man or woman in one earthly lifetime. Still, I feel strongly that God has called me to play a role—along with a growing number of Christians in the Hollywood community—in sharing the Good News of Jesus Christ through culturally relevant films with Christian content. We've begun that journey with "Livin' It," an edgy extreme sports video that follows some Christian skateboard and BMX athletes who live out their faith in a hardcore world.

Today's young people are more "connected" than ever through technology and the media, but so many are still lost. Even in the Christian community, there's a huge disconnect among the Christian media establishment, the churches, and a new generation of motivated and engaged young believers.

Matthew Turner's *The Christian Culture Survival Guide* reconnects us with spirited and often humorous musings that challenge the status quo and inspire new looks at timeless topics. Matthew writes the way I hope our movies will look—straight up ... cutting edge ... fun.

As Christians, we need to hear from people like Matthew. His stories bring to light some of the past foibles of Christianity—and Christians—that happen because we're human. You'll certainly laugh and probably relate to the subjects discussed, but don't miss the cultural and spiritual truths you'll find in these pages.

The Christian Culture Survival Guide will entertain, surprise, and energize you to get past simply "surviving" your faith and on to "livin' it."

ACKNOWLEDGEMENTS

Matthew wishes to thank: The love of my life, Jessica Nicole Schim—I can't wait to marry you. Mom, Dad, Melanie, Jim, Jill, Jenna, Kelley, Kevin, Andrew, Katelyn, Bradley, Elisabeth, and David—you are the best family in the world. God has truly blessed all of us. My best friend Daniel Eagan for your prayers and advice. My friend and manager, Rebekah Hubbell, for believing in me. Lee Steffen, for listening to my gripe and praying me through it. Lisa Tedder, for your unbelievable friendship and editorial advice. Eric DeVries, for the tiny addition. Michael Tenbrink, for understanding this story. Julie Price, for early morning coffee and blueberry muffins. Jeremy Camp, for challenging me. Valerie Summers, for the advice. Pete James, for your wisdom. Libby Brown, for your hugs. Julie Johnson—for your "compassion." Paul Canady, for your honesty. Dick and Cheryl Eagan, for letting me inside your family. Dennis and Amy Kunselman, for your love and a place to sleep. Paul and Terry Klaassan—I would not be where I am without you. Brian and Cindy Bowdren—I learned a lot from you both. Nick and Kim Serban, for being my friends. My friends at *CCM* magazine for letting me join the party for a couple of years. My favorite Starbucks baristas, Drew and Bethany, for your friendly smiles. Cameron Strang, Cara Davis, and everyone else at Relevant Media Group, for believing in this book. Lastly and most importantly, I want to thank Jesus—You are the reason I survive.

TABLE OF CONTENTS

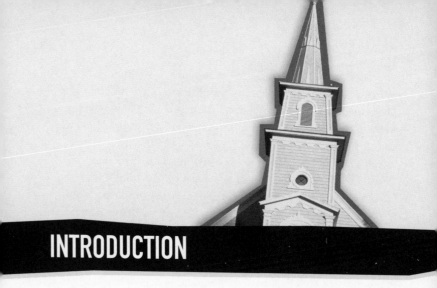

INTRODUCTION

Why do we need a Christian culture survival guide?

Because it's a crazy Christian world we live in. And it keeps getting crazier.

In the last thirty years, modern Christianity has had a substantial impact on mainstream culture. Christian consumers have gone from the fundamentalist few to a force to be reckoned with in American economy. Christian music, once regarded as the insignificant strummings of a few hippie musicians, is now a multi-million dollar industry, and many Christian distributing labels are actually owned by well-known mainstream companies such as Warner Bros. and EMI. Even Hollywood, once the throne of anti-Christian values, has ventured tentatively friendly gestures toward Christian consumers with ethical movies like *A Walk to Remember* and even overtly Christian movies like *Luther, VeggieTales,* and Mel Gibson's *The Passion of the Christ.*

Many Christians regard this gradual impact of Christian

concerns and values on mainstream culture as a good thing. And in many ways it is. But it has also given rise to one of the strangest phenomenons in the history of the Church so far. Those who live in the Christian culture refer to that phenomenon as the "Christian culture bubble."

You probably know the type. Jesus T-shirts, Christian music, WWJD bracelets, and continual references to "the Lord"—Christians who live deep in the bubble sometimes make me want to run for cover. They speak their own language of "Christianese," full of words Anglicized from first century Greek. They get excited about the latest releases from Point of Grace and Max Lucado—people who are famous in the "bubble" but unknown to the uninitiated. And they have no idea that most people who are unfamiliar with the Christian bubble have no idea what they're talking about.

I've encountered some strange stuff in Christian culture. Everything from poorly produced Passion plays to Barbie doll burnings meant to explain hell. These experiences have had a lasting influence on me. I grew up in an ultra-conservative Baptist church, studied at a liberal Christian university, and served as the editor of the leading Christian music and culture magazine. I sometimes feel like I have seen it all. Yet almost every day, new fads, trends, and travesties surface in the world of Christian culture.

I have ventured through Christian culture sometimes as a victim and sometimes as a champion, but always as an outsider. In nearly all of my experience in the Church and the hoopla (and there's a whole lot of hoopla) surrounding the Christian faith, I have often felt misplaced. I've watched many of my friends come and go in and out of faith like it's a revolving door. Sometimes they're inside the building and sometimes they're outside, and I have envied them in both instances. I have usually felt like the person stuck in the revolving door; I keep spinning around in circles, never quite sure when, where, or how to get out.

I have encountered a lot about Christian culture along the way that intrigues me and some that disgusts me to no end. Sadly, I have discovered that very little of what I have faithfully pursued for so long had much to do with knowing Jesus. Although I have been introduced to Jesus on many occasions, by hundreds of different people, places, and things, I think I have only recently truly met Him. And He's very different from what I expected Him to be. It's exciting to know that there's so much more about Him to learn and explore.

If you've recently become a believer in the Christian faith, if you've grown up in the Church but never understood the phenomenon of American Christian culture, or if you've found yourself confused when negotiating the world of church culture, then this book is for you. Having spent most of my adult life working in the Christian culture, I have had unique opportunities to observe the best and worst. I've listened to evangelists preaching the "you give and you get" prosperity doctrine that nets them up to $100 million "ministry" dollars annually. I've met followers of Jesus in third-world communities who give all they have, sleep on dirt floors, and go to bed hungry. I've met so many people who unselfishly give of their time, finances, and attention to countless needs all over the world, and I've observed first-hand the racism, sexism, and hypocrisy that decays the spiritual foundation of churches all over the world. This covers much of what I experienced, but it could hardly cover it all.

Twenty-seven years ago, I started going to church. Some of what I experienced in the church was life changing. Some of it made me laugh. Some of it made me psychotic.

Let's face it—Christians are weird. And this book is about the culture I, and perhaps you, too, encountered growing up in the Christian faith. But before you jump into the first chapter, here are a few "tips" to help you along the way.

1) You do not have to be a Christian to find this book funny. But if you would like to become a Christian before venturing forward, turn to page twenty-six. I'm kidding. Just read on.

2) Some of the stories I share about myself may seem deranged and heinous to you, which may cause you to feel sorry for me. Please do not feel sorry for me. I am on medication that helps me cope and laugh at all of the deranged and heinous things mentioned in this book.

3) No pastor, priest, or deacon was hurt during the writing of this book.

4) If you have no sense of humor, please put this book back on the shelf, coffee table, or toilet where you found it and immediately read something written by Max Lucado, Chuck Swindoll, or the Pope. You'll feel better about yourself in the morning.

5) There are no hidden messages in this book if read backwards.

6) Thou shalt not commit adultery.

7) If those of you with no sense of humor are still reading: Yes, I do passionately love Jesus and look forward to spending eternity with Him *and most of you*.

8) I do realize that in writing this book I am opening myself up to a healthy dose of ridicule, judgment, and hate mail—I was raised independent, fundamental, give-me-that-old-time-religion of hellfire and damnation Baptist—I can pretty much handle anything. But thanks for thinking about me!

9) Eat more veggies! Except for eggplant. I hate eggplant.

Here's to my first book (and perhaps my last) … I hope you enjoy!

CHAPTER 1

THE **SALVATION** EXPERIENCE

→ SOUL-WINNING MADE EASY

→ MEET JESUS EARLY

→ TELL-TALE SIGNS YOU'RE ABOUT TO HAVE AN ALTAR ENCOUNTER

→ SO WHY GET DUNKED?

THE SALVATION EXPERIENCE

Chapter 1

SUNDAY SCHOOL

Do you remember singing the song, "Oh You Can't Get To Heaven"? (*Oh, you can't get to heaven/ On roller skates/ Oh you can't get to heaven/ On roller skates/ Oh, you can't get to heaven on roller skates/ 'Cuz you'll roll right past those pearly gates!*) As a very impressionable four-year-old kid, I learned quickly that roller skates, a school bus, and a space shuttle were not in any way conducive means to get me into heaven. Of course, most of us reading this book believe or at least have heard that Christians believe only knowing Jesus as your personal Lord and Savior will get you past St. Peter and into heaven. But for a lot of us, getting the ticket to glory is the easy part; living life while having the ticket in your hand tends to be the hard part.

Everyone's salvation or "born-again" experiences are different. In my twenty-six-year history of following Jesus, I've seen people fall straight back against a hardwood floor because the preacher slammed them on the head with what he called a "Holy Spirit fist." I've watched people being pulled out of the pews and forced up the aisles to the altar. Usually, despite their initial resistance to "the Word of the Lord," their names would later be announced from the pulpit, indicating that the salvation experience had taken place. Some people would cry and scream when meeting the Lord Jesus for the first time; others would dance, shout, and run around the church like chickens. (I've always thought the whole running around the church while flapping your "wings" was for the birds.)

In 1978 Democrat and (therefore according to the church I went to) sinner Jimmy Carter was president. *Grease* star John Travolta and comedian Lily Tomlin dated for six months. *Laverne and Shirley* was one of the most popular shows on American television. And I was introduced to a lifetime commitment of following Jesus Christ as my Lord and Savior. Most people when first introduced to a relationship with Christ talk about a feeling of change, contentment, love, or at least something. I was four-years-old when I met Jesus, so the chances of me sensing an overwhelming shift in my reality were highly unlikely. I have to be honest and admit that when I first met the Lord, I didn't feel much of anything.

Back then, I always sat on the front row of my dad's Sunday school class and sang loud and clear. Even at the age of four, I treated every church service like a Broadway audition. I had a strong, melodic voice, and I sang perfectly on key. I'm sure I could have made my mom and dad a lot of money as a young singing sensation (but their opposition to that idea is a whole other story).

Dad was modest about his ability as a Sunday school teacher; "I'm just an old farm boy," he'd say. "I don't know what I'm doing." But I thought he was the most engaging storyteller I had ever heard. And Dad would never let a Sunday go by without giving us a chance to be born again.

"Now, boys," he would say at the end of every Sunday school class, "I never want you to leave this room without having an opportunity to know Jesus as your personal Lord and Savior."

Like everyone else, I was supposed to close my eyes for this part. A decision for Christ is intended to be a personal matter, unobserved by your peers. But I always peeked. While most of the boys' heads were bowed and eyes closed, I was looking around the room to see if anyone was going to raise their hand for salvation.

Will anyone respond? I wondered.

I always felt sorry for Dad when no one responded to his altar calls. I didn't really understand what it meant to know Jesus as my Lord and Savior, but it seemed so important to him.

Should I raise my hand? I thought suddenly. *I have never been saved.*

I wanted to be saved. The last thing I wanted was to spend eternity in hell.

And then, to everyone's surprise, a young man's hand went up. It was Michael, the only black kid in our Sunday school class. Michael stood up and walked slowly toward the front of the room.

The room got quiet. Suddenly I felt like I was at a big sporting event, and my dad was the star player who had just scored a "soul."

I could almost hear the sports announcer giving the play-by-play.

Look at this! Michael J. Benson is walking up the center aisle. Matthew's father has done it again. Michael's pace is slow but certain. I think he's going to do it. There is little doubt that this young man wants to know Jesus as his Lord and Savior. Look at him. He looks great, dressed in a classic white shirt and tie with black pleated pants. All the teachers are smiling. One of the volunteers is beginning to cry. Matthew's dad has just delivered one of the best salvation performances of his career. God 1, Satan 0. He's got to be excited about that …

Wait! Suddenly I felt left out, like I was missing something extraordinary. I wanted to be part of the game. *I want to get saved too!* I jumped out of my seat and ran forward to stand beside my father and Michael.

I have never seen anything like this before! Up on the opposite side of the room, another soul is fast approaching the altar. Virgil Turner will no doubt be nominated for MVP Sunday school teacher of the year for this incredible double play. The crowd is going crazy here this morning.

That makes the score: God 2, Satan 0 …

Both Michael and I prayed along with my dad, asking Jesus to come into our hearts.

MEETING JESUS IN THE EARLY YEARS

For me, meeting Jesus at an early age certainly had its privileges. First off, I was instantly perceived as one of the good kids in church. Little old ladies gave me candy. The following Sunday the pastor came to my house and drove me to Sunday night church. I didn't necessarily understand all that knowing Jesus entailed. My pastor would often equate it to having a "holy reservation" or "your ticket to glory." And even though I knew that when Jesus yelled, "All aboard!" I would get to ride on His glory train to heaven, at the age of four, I was much more impressed with the hard candy I got from the little old ladies.

However, despite the obvious privileges (candy and notoriety), meeting Jesus at the age of four also had its drawbacks. Let me explain: Most churches recognize something called the "age of accountability." Can you say "age of accountability," boys and girls? [Boys and Girls: "Age of accountability."] Although churches *are* undecided at what age an individual becomes responsible for his or her own sinful behavior, in most churches, pastors will say it's around the age of twelve. If I had known about the age of accountability ruling, I may have given the whole salvation-at-four thing at least, err, eight more years. Why? *Baptism.*

GETTING BAPTIZED—I was "dunked" of course (as opposed to "sprinkled"). Here's why it was an amazingly uncomfortable experience for me:

1) In my church, it was instantly necessary to do an out-in front-of-the-church profession of your faith through baptism—you can be dunked or sprinkled depending on your church's theological preference. My church preferred dunking! Children under twelve usually love pools and bathtubs—the big tub of water behind my church's choir loft was *not* the problem. However, wearing nothing but a blue plastic smock over my cold, skinny, naked body was humiliating—and far from spiritually transforming.

2) Compound reason number one with the fact that your hairy, overweight pastor is also wearing nothing but a plastic blue smock, leaving you with about one-one-hundreth of an inch separating you from a preacher's moist, naked body—and you have a situation that makes even the most mature twelve-year-old Baptist want to convert to Methodist or Presbyterian and opt for the more effeminate process of sprinkling. The very memory of this cruel and unusual sacrament makes me cringe.

It's easy for me to sometimes make light of baptism (I've lost count as to how many times I have actually been "raised in the likeness of his death.") However, today maturity and greater spiritual understanding have allowed me to know the importance of this particular sacrament. Baptism is a Christian's public display of faith in Jesus. It's a serious and meaningful event in one's life.

Over the last few years, I've watched many friends get baptized. For all of them, it was a sincere, life-changing experience to publicly profess their love for Christ. If you've recently become a follower of Jesus, the next official step of obedience is baptism. But before you're officially dunked or sprinkled in public, make sure you have an understanding of what this sacrament means. Ask your pastor or a spiritual mentor to explain the importance of water baptism to you. And if you decide to go the "immersion route," please wear a bathing suit. Being buck-naked underneath those blue plastic smocks that many churches make you wear is just plain SCARY!

ALTAR CALLS

Since the time of Christ's earthly ministry, millions of people have come to know the Lord—and in a thousand different ways. But no doubt, the most popular way for an old-fashioned, confess-your-sins-and-ask-Jesus-into-your-heart experience to occur is at the altar. Cleverly, the time set aside for "altar visitation" is called an altar call. Can you say "altar …" Okay, I'll stop.

The church I grew up in lived for altar calls. That invitation to come forward and be saved that my dad gave at the end of every Sunday school wasn't unusual in my church; we had one at the end of *every* service. Not a single church event—prayer meeting, outing, or potluck—could go by without one. Even on our youth trip to the zoo, before we could go see the elephants and pandas, we had to sweat it out on the sticky bus seats through a devotional and an altar call ... or I guess it was a "front of the bus" call.

The preachers who led these altar calls yelled and screamed. One couldn't help but respond—we were scared not to.

I later became aware that many people have never experienced an old-fashioned altar call. Perhaps you haven't either. Sometimes altar calls are a little scary for people, so it's always nice to know what you're getting ready to experience before it happens.

TELL-TALE SIGNS YOU'RE ABOUT TO ENCOUNTER AN "OLD-FASHIONED" MEETING WITH THE ALTAR

➡ If the pastor closes his or her sermon with, "I want every head bowed and every eye closed—I want no looking around." This sign is a biggie! My advice? Do exactly what the preacher tells you to do.

➡ If there is lots of rustling around by individuals who have "altar call" responsibilities (i.e., deacons, musicians, singers, and ushers will usually be scurrying to get into position). These people will be looking down at their feet as if you can't see them as they walk over your toes and into the aisle.

➡ If you hear the word "stanza"—*look it up.*

➡ If you hear the pastor say, "I see that hand" as he or she looks around the room for potential converts.

➡️ If the song being sung during your altar call begins with the words "just" or "all." If this happens, you are definitely in the midst of an altar call. Just hum along if you don't know the words.

The point of altar calls at church, of course, was something called "soul winning." I was taught early on that for every soul I won for the Lord, there would be a bright and shining star placed in my heavenly crown. The more souls won, the prettier my crown. It's not like I completely believed them, but I *had* tried to convince my best friend Julie to be born again, but her mom and dad wouldn't let her.

SOUL WINNING

Here's a quick explanation of how my church "won souls." (All churches work a little differently.)

When a "new dead soul" (NDS) walked through the doors at our church, his or her presence initiated a carefully orchestrated soul-winning procedure designed to ensure the best possible odds for a quick and effortless soul conversion. Souls were converted weekly at our church services, and our conversion rate was outstanding.

A first-time visitor was labeled as an NDS using preliminary information gathered by the head usher. He would find out the individual's name, age, sex, and current church membership. The usher would then make the call on whether the individual qualified for NDS status. The NDS was escorted to the first available pew, as close as possible to the front of the church. The usher would then notify one of the church pastors about the assumed NDS and where he would be sitting.

At that point, the NDS was allowed to enjoy most of the service in peace—but only until the pastor began his invitation. Once the altar call started, the NDS was fair game for proselytizing by any willing church leader. During the invitation, all of the pastors and any attending deacons were asked to come up front. Much like the sales people at department stores who bother you when you're just trying to browse through a rack of clothes, it was nearly impossible to go to the altar and pray without one of the leaders asking you if you needed their assistance. But of course, an NDS, being a "dead" soul, wouldn't have been able to *really* pray without assistance anyway.

In order to provide ample opportunity for any NDS to respond, our altar calls were always relentlessly long. The length of an altar call is measured not in minutes or hours, but in stanzas—the time it takes to complete a verse and chorus of the hymn of invitation. If the NDS had not responded to the pastor's message by the second stanza, a pastor or deacon would usually leave his post by the altar to stand next to the NDS and whisper in his ear.

"Do you know where you would go if you were to die today?" the pastor would ask the NDS. Then he would add in a friendly tone, "I can walk forward with you, and in just one stanza you'll know *exactly* where you're going when you die."

If the church leader was a good "soulsman," it would usually only take a couple of minutes to convince the NDS to walk forward. Then, while the NDS was taken through the five-point plan of salvation by one of the church-approved witnesses on duty, the church leader was free to go look for another NDS.

Our NDS conversion rate was usually around 62 percent (estimated). So there was nearly a two-thirds chance that any NDS who came to our church would be converted to a New Living Soul (NLS) by the end of the service. If the NDS became a NLS, he or she would then be baptized, encouraged to join the church, and invited to teach Sunday school (well, maybe not on the first Sunday).

Soul winning was a way of life in the church I went to. Every week, we had days set aside for going door-to-door through the community, stopping at every house in search of a poor losing soul who needed salvation. Unfortunately, the church often took soul winning too far. In fact, some people were just all-out strange in their determination to win as many souls as possible. I remember talking to a young couple that had actually joined a "Save-A-Soul-A-Day" campaign. A team of twelve couples made a pact that they as a group would save one soul a day every day for a year. One of these couples was spending a holiday at my family's house when they received an emergency phone call from another member of their group. Apparently, no one in the group had saved a soul yet that day. Three of the twelve couples were out on "emergency duty," going from house to store to restaurant looking for an unsaved soul willing to pray the sinner's prayer. My friends were preparing to leave my house early and drive an hour back to their hometown as reinforcements when the phone rang again. One of the other members of the group had just walked into a McDonald's and convinced someone to pray the prayer of salvation. Whew! That was a close call!

Today, I think forced proselytizing causes much harm for the kingdom of God. Yet sadly, we have become a Christian society offering a "fast food" mentality on salvation—get everyone through the line as quickly as possible and hope they order a combo. This isn't evangelism. This is a cheap, franchised form of Christianity that churches today still try to utilize to bring people to Jesus. I have a sincere desire for all people to hear the saving message of Jesus Christ, but I've learned that building relationships is the key, not crazy one-a-day plans to ensure people say the words of the sinner's prayer.

If salvation truly is the most important decision that an individual can make, and I firmly believe it is, then Christians need to be wiser about of how we go about telling people about Jesus. The son of God is the most compelling, attractive, and offensive individual to have ever walked on earth, and He spent time building relationships with people. It's extremely important for the Church to connect with the lost, but sometimes our current "get everybody to the altar" tactics aren't doing it. In order to reach people, we need authentic lovers of Christ willing to walk through the trenches and meet people in their personal habitat. The Apostle Paul said it best in 1 Corinthians 9:19-23: "For though I am free from all men, I have made myself a slave to all, so that I may win more. To the Jews I became as a Jew, so that I might win Jews; to those who are under the Law, as under the Law though not being myself under the Law, so that I might win those who are under the Law; to those who are without law, as without law, though not being without the law of God but under the law of Christ, so that I might win those who are without law. To the weak I became weak, that I might win the weak; I have become all things to all men, so that I may by all means save some. I do all things for the sake of the gospel, so that I may become a fellow partaker of it."

CHAPTER 2

THE **CHURCH**

→ CAN YOU FIND THE RIGHT ONE FOR YOU?

→ FIFTEEN TYPES OF CHURCH PEOPLE TO LOOK OUT FOR

→ CHURCH HOPPING ESSENTIALS

THE CHURCH
Chapter 2

CHOOSING A CHURCH

Once you've met Jesus, the next task that Christians usually venture out and do is discovering a church that is right for them. The unfortunate part about giving advice on finding a church is that the selection varies greatly from state to state and even from town to town. California, Texas, Florida, and Tennessee seem to offer a wide selection of churches, differing by denomination, worship style, and size. However, other states, such as Montana and Arkansas, offer a healthy number of churches, but it's hard differentiating the distinct characteristics between each separate house of God. But in most major cities, the number of churches is growing weekly, so keep checking the phone book for new churches popping up around your town.

When I was a child, I didn't have a choice of where to attend church. I went to church where my parents told me to go. By associating myself with my parents, I was instantly identified as an independent, fundamental, "you're-going-to-hell-if-you're-not-Baptist" Baptist. Sadly, it wasn't the grandest spiritual experience. My church was legalistic and judgmental. I quickly learned that my church wasn't the only legalistic religious establishment. Many churches seem to have a perpetual need to rule over people. This kind of church exists everywhere and in every denomination. I have slowly learned over the years that for my faith's survival, I have to turn around and face my past—although bleak, this includes my spiritual past.

During the '60s, '70s, and early '80s, fundamentalist churches flourished in the United States and around the world. Devout followers of God fell in love with old-fashioned hellfire and brimstone preaching, made famous by the eighteenth-century preacher Jonathan Edwards in his classic sermon, "Sinners in the Hands of an Angry God." Street preachers, evangelists, and pastors all around the world imitated Edwards' tactics in an effort to "scare the living hell" out of non-believers and drive them to the altar to receive Jesus. My church was founded on these kinds of principles, and consequently, I had the privilege of growing up in a rule-oriented religious establishment that more times than not stole my freedom away from me. To just graze the surface, here are a few of the rules my church expected us to follow. There was to be:

No dancing, gyrating, head bopping, or (in church) clapping.

No drinking, smoking, cursing, or hanging around those who did do these things.

No watching the *Smurfs*, *He-Man*, the *Care Bears*, or *Jem*.

No watching *The Cosby Show*, *Laverne and Shirley*, *The Facts of Life*, *Dukes of Hazard*, or *TJ Hooker*.

No playing with or publicly displaying unicorns, wizards, gnomes, elves, or any other fantasy creatures. (One member of my church actually thought rhinoceroses should be considered unicorns and therefore refused to let his child go to the zoo's rhino house.)

No touching, holding hands, hugging, or kissing the opposite sex. (I *think* this rule was waived for married couples …) No friendships or relationships of any kind with those who were "lost" (i.e., not members of our church).

And there were hundreds more …

Although these rules sound rigid, ridiculous, and completely insane to me now, my family stood behind every one of them back then. Nearly every Sunday, my pastor made a point to re-emphasize church rules to the congregation, making them near impossible to forget.

Throughout my Christian life, I questioned the rules of my church and knew I didn't fit in. Heck, I sometimes felt like I walking through a bad episode of *The Twilight Zone*. But I had no idea how to remedy my situation. Yet despite my dilemma, I remained a freethinker with a strong desire to know God, and I was determined that no church, pastor, or legalistic fanatic was going to keep me from knowing the *real* Jesus. And the same goes for you.

CHURCH PEOPLE TO WATCH OUT FOR

FIFTEEN KINDS OF CHURCH PEOPLE TO LOOK OUT FOR

1 **Know-it-all Bible nerds**—These Scripture-quoting maniacs often prefer King James to Eugene Peterson. They whiz through Bible trivia and Charles Stanley books like it's their job, and have a hard time differentiating between the earthly and the heavenly. Prone to lacking personalities, these individuals usually huddle together on the left or right side of the church auditorium, sharing biblical knowledge, contemplating apologetics, and becoming stranger with every passage memorized. They are also the individuals who as children kick everyone's butts at the Bible quiz meets and *always* win the sword drills.

2   **The really, *really* nice old ladies**—Watch out for those sickeningly sweet, pudgy old ladies who sit in the back of the auditorium and woo you in with their free Mentos and tender "God bless you, sweeties." Those ladies may come across like they don't know what they're doing, but secretly they wield a great deal of influence and are sharper than nails.

3   **Overly enthusiastic church welcomers**—There is something a little alarming about middle-aged women who give you full frontal hugs as soon as you walk through the front door of the church. It's always nice to see a pleasant face, but over-the-top exuberance can sometimes turn people away.

4   **The rubberneckers**—Always looking around to see who's in church or what people are doing, the rubbernecker can be very annoying—especially, when you're sitting behind him. When I see people doing this, I want to hit them upside their heads.

5   **Praise team rock star**—Flashy big hair, flamboyant guitars, and fancy footwork are key characteristics of the praise team rockster. Always a treat to watch, the hip worshiper has a Crest-whitened smile, *GQ* good looks, and a righteous ability to bring himself into the presence of people.

6   **The hippie pastor**—Former longhaired, lovemaking drug addicts, these pastors now wear Birkenstock sandals, khakis, and plaid long-sleeve shirts and talk passionately about grace and unconditional love. Although known for using the more touchy feely faith language from the stage, hippie pastors find it difficult to relate to many in their congregations, so they spend more time studying Scripture than interacting with people.

7 **Hardcore hand raiser praiser**—In most cases, hardcore praisers sit in the front row or on the pew ends (aisle usage is a complete possibility) so they can dance, wave their hands, and yell out spiritual proclamations for others to hear. Usually, the presence of God seemingly finds these people as soon as the first chord of "Trading My Sorrows" is played and doesn't stop until the pastor's closing "amen."

8 **Brother so-and-so**—Always referring to his church peeps as brother fill-in-the-blank, those who fit into the "brother so-and-so" category are often the more annoying of church-going individuals—although they're the first people to invite you to an after-church lunch with friends or family, they are also the first ones you'll end up trying to avoid when church is finished. Known for giving firm hand shakes and asking uncomfortable spiritual questions, brother so-and-so will try to become your closest friend—and he's likely been close friends with nearly every other member of the church. My advice? Create healthy boundaries.

9   **Geeky elders**—These men and women are easy to spot. Just look for the man with a bad comb over or the woman wearing the modest, bibbed sundress with an elastic-waist, then find their spouses, and they're the geeky elders. You'll often see them counting church attendees from the back or inconspicuously from the aisle-ways. More often than not, these people are some of the nicest people you'll ever meet and are extremely helpful when you're questioning something about the church.

10   **Perfect church family**—If you can imagine a nice-looking husband with the six-figure job, a doting, plain-dressed mother who insists on home schooling her children, an eerily polite seven-year-old girl who often corrects her hyperactive four-year-old brother, and the perfect never-crying infant, and you have a pretty good idea of the "perfect church family."

11   **The zany, Abercrombie and Fitch-looking youth minister dude**—Complete with an urbanesque/surfer-style way of talking—"Yo, dude, that's off the hook, you gotz d' bling bling fo sho"—mothers actually allow this handsome twenty-six-going-on-fourteen-year-old man to be responsible for their teenagers at youth group functions—even international youth functions. Easily mistaken as just another one of the kids, you can usually spot the "leader" if you look for the "kid" with the forming beer gut or receding hairline.

12   **Token minority attendee**—Mainly found in conservative churches with mostly-white congregations, it's not uncommon to notice one or two individuals (usually from Uganda, Kenya, or Sudan) that because of their accents, nationality, and skin tone, stick out like sore thumbs. Consequently, due to the mere "adventure" of encountering and befriending a man of international status, those in the church of the Caucasian persuasion make this African attendee one of the most popular people in the church.

13   **Pastor's wife**—Though seemingly meek and patient, you never want to tick off the pastor's wife. She is the glue that holds the man of God's sanity together. If you come between her and her man, you discover rage like that of a hurricane or tornado. Although she may have a half-used bottle of Prozac in her medicine closet, don't let her tendency for mental and emotional breakdowns fool you. She knows exactly what's going on and will have you figured out faster than she can say, "Welcome to our church, sweetie!"

14   **The desperate male divorcee**—Having lived without the love of a woman for at least seven years, this middle-aged, "nicest guy in the world but always on the prowl" divorcee has tried to date every single, available woman in the church. Usually in the midst of a ten-year bout with a mid-life crisis, this regular church attendee can't seem to ever shake the guilt of his partying days. With a name that is usually something like "Tony," "Barry," or "Tex," the desperate male divorcee never stays in one church for more than two or three years.

15 **Homecoming queen**—Beautiful. Godly. A perfect inescapable vision for the single Christian male. The "homecoming queen" is a goddess in her own little world. She's her own religion with all-male followers. She's not considered pious, yet she's mysteriously confident. You'll spot her sitting with the rest of her peers trying to fit in, but with every step, every flip of her golden blonde hair, she sets herself apart from the other girls in the church. However, she usually marries the church jock right out of high school, has three kids before she turns twenty-five, and is depressed, frumpy, and singing in the church choir before thirty. *So wake up, guys!*

CURRENT CHURCH TRENDS

I have visited many churches in my search of the right one for me. Notice, I use the word "right" and not "perfect." Perfect churches do not exist. I'm convinced of that. If you think you are attending a perfect church, just give it some time. You'll get hit over the head with some kind of bad religious surprise eventually. I think I've seen it all. I've been splashed with holy water during a Catholic mass, yelled and screamed at at a Baptist church, watched others parade the aisles mimicking ducks at a Pentecostal service, wept tears of boredom at a Lutheran church, and sweated to death at a non-denominational church that met in a non-air-conditioned gymnasium. And I survived it all with only a few spiritual scrapes and bruises.

There is actually a term for people like me. An individual who goes from church to church to church is called a "church hopper." It's usually considered a derogatory term, but I have learned the hard way that there is an art to church hopping in today's over-saturated church market.

Armed with a small, concealed bottle of Advil—I don't recommend church hopping without some kind of stash of headache medicine—I've visited nearly fifty different churches over the last two years. It's much harder work than I realized! The insane amounts of junk mail, phone calls, and requests for money alone were enough to send me over the edge.

IN THE MERE FIFTY OR SO CHURCHES I VISITED, HERE ARE SIX INTERESTING THINGS I OBSERVED:

1) Today's church trend seems to be moving toward lengthier services. It's not unusual these days for a preacher to expound on Scripture for more than an hour—which is a little long for me. When I was a kid, even my Baptist preachers knew when it was time to shut up and go home.

2) Synchronized dancing seems to be a growing movement as well. I have no problem with laypeople breaking out their moves during a service, but a worship team-led dance instruction class was too much like watching reruns of *American Bandstand* on VH1.

3)   Twice I have been sitting in a church and suddenly
been frightened by loud booming voices and haphazard
clapping coming from the rear of the balcony. It was the
choir. In a new twist on an old tradition, churches are
putting the choir behind the congregation. Why wouldn't
they do that with the pastor too?

4)   One service I visited was actually a live broadcast from a
church more than an hour and a half away. We didn't
participate in the service; we watched it via satellite on a
big screen TV. It made me think that a one-world church
service can't be that far away.

5)   Pastors say all sorts of weird and unexpected things. I heard
one pastor, during a sermon about circumcision, make
continuous penis jokes. The congregation responded with
awkward silence, but the pastor wouldn't take a hint.
Another pastor spoke proudly about his church's diverse
congregation. He referred to the piano player as an
example. "The guy who played piano this morning," this
pastor announced smugly, "has a *nose* ring! How about
that?" How *about* that?

6)   Another pastor warned his congregation not to treat the
C-level "celebrities" who frequented their church any
differently from anyone else. He reminded them that
celebrities are just people like you and me; they need a
comfortable place to worship. Two minutes later, this

same pastor announced, "One of our faithful members, Billy Ray Cirrus, will be performing for our Christmas Eve service this year. You may want to invite your friends!" *Hey, friend! Remember in the early '90s when Billy Ray Cirrus was cool? Wanna come hear him play in my church on Christmas Eve?*

DON'T GO CHURCH HOPPING WITHOUT SIX THINGS

1 **Headache medicine**—As mentioned earlier, you'll want to have a bottle of Tylenol, Advil, or Excedrin Migraine with you at all times.

2 **Tennis shoes**—Normally, people wear dress shoes to church, but in some churches, you'll be jumping up and down so much, you'll feel like you're taking an aerobics class with the Holy Spirit.

3 **Bible**—Don't rely on the cheesy church bulletins to provide you with the correct Scripture, take your Bible to church. Don't you know that the Bible is your sword?! Why would you even think about going to war without your weapon? I would hate to see you show up on the frontlines of heaven with a bulletin in your hand.

4 **Sense of humor**—If you go church hopping, you're going to hear some really funny things, so get ready to laugh. Be prepared for anything!

5   **Address book**—You'll no doubt meet tons of new people. Whether or not you decide to join that church, get the names and numbers of people you meet at each church. You never know when you may want to ask one of them out on a date.

6   **Voice recorder**—Just in case you write your own book someday about your church hopping experiences, you may want a way to remember all of your adventures.

THIS IS IN THE BIBLE?

"If that person still refuses to listen, take your case to the church. If the church decides you are right, but the other person won't accept it, treat that person as a pagan or a corrupt tax collector." —Matthew 18:17

THE NO-CHURCH CHURCH?

Recently, I visited a non-denominational church with a dear friend of mine. He had been asking me to attend for quite some time, so somewhat half-heartedly I accepted his invitation. Have you noticed that in many of today's church services, the pastors are seemingly trying to make you think that their church is not your daddy's religion? Well, such was the case with the minister of my friend's church.

The pastor had this strange resemblance to Lumbergh from the movie *Office Space*. He stood on the stage in a large live-music venue, using a fifty-gallon drum as his makeshift pulpit. The very first words out of his mouth were, "If you're here to experience church, you've come to the wrong place." My heart fluttered with excitement for a split second. I love worship services that tend to be different, or at least creative.

He continued, "We don't have church here at Middletown Community …"

We then proceeded to indeed *have* church. And it was just like my daddy's church. No, seriously, it was. We sang hymns and praise songs. We heard a sermon. The worship leaders raised their hands and shouted, "Praise You, Jesus," during the instrumental parts. There was absolutely nothing I experienced at Middletown Community that was *not* church. For me, this is fine, but why did the pastor stand up and give a speech about his church not being church?

Today's churches seem to be experiencing a pretty substantial identity crisis. I truly believe that churches like Middletown know what they want out of their worship service, but have no idea how to get there. There is nothing wrong with having "old fashioned" church, but don't try to trick me into thinking that it's not what it is. If there's singing, preaching, and an offering, chances are, it's a church.

Fellowship, worship, and spiritual growth among other lovers of Christ is very important. I do believe many churches have lost their vision and purpose; however, one's involvement in a local church body is an essential part of a Christian's maturity. I go to church because I like going to a particular place and worshiping God with my friends and family. But I do want to be clear, church DOES NOT in any way define my relationship with Christ. It enhances my relationship, but I believe our personal interaction with Christ on an ongoing basis is what sustains me as a follower of Christ.

THE **PASTOR**

→ FIVE QUESTIONS YOU NEVER WANT A PASTOR TO ASK

→ THREE STEREOTYPICAL ASSUMPTIONS TO KNOW

→ EIGHT WAYS TO KNOW YOU'RE WORSHIPING THE PASTOR

→ FIVE PASTORS TO LOOK OUT FOR

THE PASTOR

Chapter 3

Choosing the pastor that is right for you is something like picking the perfect ripe melon at the supermarket. I'm not kidding. When you're choosing a sweet honeydew melon or a mouthwatering cantaloupe, you look for a firm shell, yet a soft, succulent middle. The same is true for a pastor. You want him or her to be solid and confident on the outside, but compassionate and digestible on the inside. And just like melons, you want your pastor to be ripe, but certainly not too ripe. Over-ripened *anything* is not edible or fit to keep around. But unlike looking for the perfect melon, where there are times when the shopping is at least enjoyable, finding a pastor that is right for you is hard, not very much fun, and sometimes near-impossible.

THREE STEREOTYPICAL ASSUMPTIONS TO KNOW WHEN SEARCHING FOR A PASTOR

1 An over-zealous pastor is usually hiding something. Now of course, in some cases, he or she may just be suffering from excessive intakes of caffeine. However, more often than not, if the pastor is too over-the-top excited about your visit, he's been hurt in the past and suffers from a great amount of emotional "flocked-up" baggage. Just worship in caution.

2   A pastor who does not open his or her Bible during a sermon could be a false prophet. The New Testament warning clearly states that in the last days, there will be many false teachers among us, so you need to be pretty darn positive that you're not sitting in the flock of one of them and partaking in their false teachings. Just worship with your eyes open.

3   If the pastor has a shaved head, often wears white, powdery makeup, and frequently talks about space shuttles, you may want to visit a new church.

When you're visiting churches, meeting a new pastor every other week can be awkward. It's kind of like going up to someone else's father and telling them, "I want to be parented by you today, so I decided to come to your house." The pastor has no idea why you're attending his or her church. But no matter what your reason for visiting, you can usually count on a super-friendly welcome from a pastor when you attend his church for the first time. But keep in mind that just because a pastor is super-friendly on your first visit, it takes months before you can really know and trust a pastor. I recommend in all "spiritual" decision-making to take things slow. Do not rush into a "relationship" until you're completely sure of your commitment.

I think determining your involvement with a new church pastor is supposed to be a lot like a healthy dating relationship—passion, attraction, and compatibility grow slowly over time. But I'm the kind of guy who tends to fall in love fast. And with one pastor in particular, I fell "in love" too fast. And I paid for it dearly in the end.

I had decided to visit a small church about an hour from where I was living at the time. At first, I was not overly wowed. The church service was pretty good. I mean, the praise and worship band consisted of *four* rhythm guitar players playing the Jewish-influenced praise song "Jehovah Jireh" in two different keys at the same time, but it was actually pretty entertaining. What with the music and the strange synchronized clapping that is more commonly heard at Bar Mitzvahs, I kind of felt like I was at a Passover celebration. Still, the pastor seemed oddly authentic. And by the time I listened to the pastor speak and was greeted by him afterward, there was no doubt that I'd be coming back.

I fell in love with the church and its pastor practically overnight. And despite my complete foreknowledge about my issues with "church and pastoral relationships," I dove headfirst into an obsessive "spiritual" affair with a pastor I barely knew. And because I loved and respected the pastor so much, I quickly got involved with the church. I joined the "college and career" Sunday school class. I taught "little church" for the kids. I met with the pastor to drink gourmet coffees and teas at a fancy Christian coffeehouse. I joined a group of guys for another accountability group. I sang in the choir. I volunteered with youth group activities. My newfound church relationship ended up being more like one big orgy of activities, friendships, pride, and ignorance.

But eventually the little church with the amazing pastor fell apart. Due to irreconcilable differences with the pastor, families started leaving the church. It certainly wasn't entirely the pastor's fault, but nonetheless I had to come to grips with the fact the man of God whom I loved dearly was not all he claimed to be. That was hard.

I thought I had learned over the years not to rush into relationships too quickly. But obviously, I still had some learning to do. Just remember, when you're visiting churches and meeting pastors, don't rush into things. The relationship you have with the man or woman who will be guiding you spiritually is much too important to be taken lightly. So take things slow. You'll be so glad you did.

DON'T EVEN THINK TO ASK ME THAT

FIVE QUESTIONS YOU NEVER WANT A PASTOR TO ASK ON THE FIRST SUNDAY

1. "What did you think of my sermon this morning, young man?"—One pastor from Tacoma Park, Maryland, asked me this question. I looked at him very nonchalantly and said, "What sermon?"

2. "So do you think you'll be coming back next Sunday?" This question sounds desperate. If you ever have a pastor ask you this, respond very excitedly with your own question: "Are you going to be preaching?" Then just walk away.

3. "Do you believe in tithing?" I must say, I have never been asked this particular question, but a friend of mine has, and I can certainly see why he didn't go to that particular church again.

4   "Can I come visit you sometime this week?" NO!

5   "You want to step into my office?" Not on the first visit.

A lot of churches today have gotten so big that the pastor has a hard time remembering people's names. I've heard my current pastor forget the name of a young lady he was baptizing and the names of a young husband and wife who had decided to join his church. I've actually introduced myself to my pastor five times, and he has forgotten my name every single time. He even forgets my face; it's like I'm a visitor every time I see him. I finally stopped introducing myself. He has no idea that I have been a "first-time visitor" at his church every Sunday for more than a year. But to be honest, I kind of like it that way. For most of my life, the pastors who have known me usually wind up disappointing me. However, it wasn't always like that.

NAMETAG SUNDAY

If you've been visiting a church for more than six months and the pastor happens to forget your name during "hand-shaking time," smile real big and kindly offer him your nametag.

My parents sure were impressed the first time we met the pastor of our first church. He was a "preacher boy," as he liked to be called, from the Midwest. Having just graduated with a degree in pastoral studies from an independent, fundamental Baptist college near Chicago, this preacher boy felt that God had called him to our hometown to start a church.

He knocked on our door on August 14, 1977, one of the hottest days of the summer.

The preacher boy, Nolan, was maybe twenty-two, twenty-three years old. He was wearing a long-sleeved dress shirt, tan pants, and a wide polyester tie. He sat stiffly on our brown tweed couch, legs crossed like a girl and hands clasped around a cup of decaf coffee.

"Hey, young man," he greeted me.

The pastor was balding badly. He did his best to hide it by letting one side grow really long and then combing it over to the other. But it didn't work at all, and it was the first thing I noticed about him.

Mom must have seen that I was staring oddly at the preacher's head, because she spoke up quickly.

Pastor wasn't really fat, but he was far from skinny. At first I thought his neck was missing, because it looked as though his head was sitting right on his shoulders. Later I realized that was because he was slouching so badly.

"Hello, I'm Matthew," I said, reaching out to give him my best handshake, making sure the skin between my pointer finger and my thumb met his before I launched into my grip. Anything less would have come across as limp and might have made him think I was a "funny." My dad had taught me the value of a good solid handshake.

"Nice grip for a kid your age," he said, winking at me, and combing his fingers through my thick hair.

"Thank you," I said politely.

Mom and Dad talked with him for hours about their displeasure with the teaching at the Methodist church, where we were members at the time.

"There's no mention of salvation through Jesus," said Dad, "and I don't feel like my family is growing spiritually in the church we go to now."

Pastor nodded empathetically and started talking about his vision for a church in our community that would emphasize Jesus first. He spoke fast and smooth, like a salesman giving a pitch. He even wore his slogan on a bright gold tiepin that read "Jesus First."

"I believe I am going to grow a great work of God," he concluded, taking his glasses off and rubbing his eyes again. "But I need your help, Virgil. Will you and Carole consider joining my church?"

"We will pray about it, preacher," my dad promised.

And as Mom waved that pudgy, bald-headed, beady-eyed, slick-talking preacher boy out the door, she wore a big, toothy grin like the Cheshire Cat. There was no doubt she was sold on the idea of attending the new Baptist church. But Dad always did say that Mom could be convinced to buy a mad dog if it was on sale.

As a child, I didn't realize how pivotal a moment this was going to be in my life. Little did I realize how much a pastor defines the culture of a church and how that culture would ultimately alter *my* life and the lives of so many others.

Some pastors, priests, evangelists, and reverends have little clue how deeply an impact they have on the lives of those in their congregations. It's uncanny how much emphasis and emotional weight I placed on my mere interactions with those who were in spiritual leadership over my life. As a child, pastors and traveling evangelists were like celebrities to me. When the pastor announced that one of our denomination's famous preachers was coming for a week of revival meetings, I would practically wriggle in my pew with excitement. By the time I was twelve years old, the opening pages of my A.V. 1611 King James Version Holy Bible were covered with autographs from my favorite preachers and evangelists. They were always happy to give me their autographs, just like real celebrities.

EIGHT WAYS TO KNOW IF YOU MIGHT BE WORSHIPING YOUR PASTOR

1 If you have ever taken a "sharpie" with you to church on Sunday morning.

2 If you look around during "closing prayer" for the quickest route to where the pastor will be after the service.

3 If you own two or more books written by your pastor.

4 If you have your pastor's cell phone on speed dial.

5 If you've ever caught yourself picking out your Sunday outfit based on a previous compliment from your reverend.

6 If you have a special CD holder for *his* sermons only.

7   If you travel more than an hour to church on Sunday morning.

8   If you have ever skipped Sunday mornings because you know your pastor is out of town.

The *popular* pastors I have known, just like many other individuals who undeservingly get put on pedestals, struggle with pride, have quirky desires for attention, and often misuse their influence. Ego and idol-worship are a dangerous combination when one considers that the men and women who lead a church or parish have the responsibility of leading a congregation of God lovers closer to humility, mercy, and meekness. In churches all across the world, we have pastors who act more like entertainers and politicians than practicing men and women of God. This kind of behavior leads to a type of humanism called people worship. One of the churches I attended when I was twenty years old was notorious for worshiping the pastor. However, scarier yet was our love, respect, and worship of the man who helped launch our denomination. His name was Jack Files.

KEY VERSES TO KNOW

"How then will they call on Him in whom they have not believed? How will they believe in Him whom they have not heard? And how will they hear without a preacher?"
—Romans 10:14

In 1991, Jack Files was probably the meanest and most self-centered preacher of his day, and he was proud of it. My entire denomination loved him. He preached it hard and fast, and that's how his congregation liked it. My parents, like most members of our church, had hundreds of Jack's sermons on cassettes.

Nothing in the worldly culture of our day was off-limits from Jack's hard-nosed preaching. He warned continually of impending judgment. "God will intervene and spare this nation," he proclaimed, "when His people are sanctified; when Christian ladies turn off the soap operas; when Christian young people forsake their rock music; when Christian ladies learn to dress modestly; when a liberal is a liberal again and a fundamentalist is a fundamentalist again; when right is right, wrong is wrong, black is black and white is white again; when God's men are prophets again; when we again hear sermons on judgment, hell, drinking, dancing, and gambling; when fundamentalists sing like fundamentalists, talk like fundamentalists, and dress like fundamentalists again; and when we get back to our sawdust-trail, mourner's-bench Christianity which preaches holy living from the pulpit and practices it in the pulpit and the pew! Let us fight abortion. Let us fight the liquor traffic. Let us fight communism. Let us fight the dirty television shows. Let us fight homosexuality!"

FIVE TYPES OF PASTORS TO LOOK OUT FOR

1 **Pastor of Politics**—If your pastor reminds you more of Ted Kennedy or Newt Gingrich than Billy Graham, you have a serious problem.

2　**Doctrine Man**—If your pastor seems to place more emphasis on proving his theology correct than preaching the name of Jesus, find a new church.

3　**End Times Fanatic**—A pastor being somewhat intrigued about what's going to happen in the future is one thing, but basing your entire church on the book of Revelation is another.

4　**Career Pastor**—If your pastor acts more like the church's CEO than he does a man trying to help and encourage you spiritually, you may want to visit somewhere else.

5　**Control Freak**—A pastor consumed with rules will lead you far from the grace and mercy of Jesus Christ.

We didn't have a choice whether to like Jack or not. His followers and admirers surrounded us. Everyone in my church yearned to be just like Jack. Every one of our pastors came from Jack's college and most of the high school seniors in our church went to his college. Whatever Jack's church did, we did. Because, to us, Jack was always right. He was the like the godfather of our denomination.

But as a young adult, I never cared much for Jack Files. He was a freak of nature. He seemed to think he was the second-best thing to Jesus. And I just couldn't quite buy into that.

Nevertheless, our church became sold out for Jack. The rich members of my church sent money to Jack and his causes. Our pastor made sure every new assistant pastor who came to our church came directly from Jack's college. Our church's Christian school was filled with teachers from Jack's church. Nearly every student who graduated from that school between the years of 1981 and 1984 went off to Jack's college. Many of them later returned to our church to work.

But our little church was just one of hundreds of fundamentalist Baptist churches in the United States filled with regular people who firmly believed that Jack Files was this country's modern savior, and no one in my small town Baptist church could be convinced otherwise.

Believe it or not, I learned a lot from Jack—but most of it was what *not* to do.

There are a lot of Jack-type preachers in Christian culture. Most of them don't have all the crazy ideals that Jack Files pursued, but they do have the self-inflated ego that they use to wield power, arrogance, and financial wealth.

IT'S ALL ABOUT ME

SIX SIGNS YOUR PASTOR MIGHT HAVE AN EGO PROBLEM

1 Instead of regular spoken announcements, your pastor stars in his own pre-recorded commercials that advertise the Bible study he'll be teaching on Wednesday nights.

2 Your pastor not only preaches the sermons, but he's also the vocal-savvy praise and worship leader, saxophone soloist, and the church's self-proclaimed comedy relief.

3   Your pastor's fashion sense brings to mind a Banana Republic minimum-waged employee rather than a slightly overweight southern politician.

4   Your pastor has read from his own book during his one of his sermons.

5   Your pastor has a booking agent, publicity representative, and his own stylist.

6   Your pastor is a member of Hair Club for Men, is a self-described metrosexual, does most of his "ministering" while at the gym, or can't walk by a Sunglass Hut without at least going inside.

Definitely watch out for the pastor with an "ego." An ego and religious influence is a very dangerous combination.

THE VALUE OF A PASTOR

I met a young pastor while I was in college a few years back who took me under his spiritual wing and taught me what it truly means to follow Jesus. We had lunch together on several occasions. During these chats, he let me talk about my problems. He let me be the real me. His humility and wisdom astounded me. I had never met a pastor quite like him, and I grew closer to my Savior because of his influence in my life.

An honest, heartfelt relationship between a lay person and a pastor is so important. You should feel comfortable addressing anything and everything with the man or woman who is leading your church. A good, kind, loving pastor can offer insight and biblical wisdom that will help you make wise and godly decisions. Sadly, I've only had the pleasure of meeting a few pastors whom I trusted and loved. But those few men and women have had a profound impact on my life. And I believe you too, will find spiritual strength in a healthy, strong relationship with you pastor.

CHAPTER 4

CHURCH
INVOLVEMENT

→ HOW TO VOLUNTEER FOR JESUS

→ A COUPLE TRUTHS YOU SHOULD KNOW

→ HOW TO BE MORE THAN A VOLUNTEER

→ FIVE BENEFITS OF MULTICHURCHING

CHURCH INVOLVEMENT
Chapter 4

So you've found Jesus and settled into a comfortable church that has a pastor who majors in humility, but I hate to break it to you—you're just getting started. I know what you're thinking, *What could possibly be next?* Well, I'll tell you! You have the over-hyped responsibility of trying to fit in to your new God environment by blending in with the Christian natives. Oh, I know we dress funny and talk in a language that is sometimes difficult to understand, but you have to do it. Believe me, "blending" with a new church can sometimes be difficult and overwhelming, so be emotionally prepared for just about anything.

A couple of years ago, I decided I was going to ask my church if I could volunteer for the children's ministry. There were always a lot of kids running around, and they were constantly making announcements in church that they needed more assistants. After church one Sunday, I ventured to the "children's" section of the building and asked if I could speak with the lady who was in charge. The lady I was speaking with picked up her walkie-talkie—yes, they had hand-held walkie-talkies—but was unable to reach her boss.

I stood there for about fifteen minutes, and finally the volunteer "boss" came running over to the small place where I was told to stand. Kids were running around. Babies were crying. It was quite a pathetic scene.

I told the lady I was interested in volunteering with the children's ministry.

She looked at me and asked, "Have you ever worked in kids'

ministry before?"

"No," I said, rather embarrassed.

"Well," she said somewhat condescendingly, "You're going to need to fill out this application, have a meeting with the pastor, and then be approved by the elder board. After we get confirmation from the church, we'll have to do a background check on you and get you fingerprinted. The entire process will take about four to six weeks."

What? Four to six weeks? No wonder they needed volunteers. Who has the energy to go through that kind of application process just to work for free, once a month, on Sunday mornings? Much to the surprise of the "boss," I declined on the paperwork and told her I would pray about my decision to volunteer.

Yet despite the hoops some churches have their volunteers endure before they can give freely of their time for the good, Christian work of Jesus Christ, the easiest way to blend in and actually meet other people is definitely to volunteer. You'll no doubt be asked to volunteer for something eventually, so either be prepared with a good "how-do-I-get-myself-out-of-this" excuse or grab a broom and start sweeping.

EIGHT OF THE MOST POPULAR WAYS OF VOLUNTEERING FOR JESUS INSIDE THE CHURCH

1) **Opening up your house for small group meetings—** Small groups usually meet at the more-ritzier homes of the church members. Don't expect this to be an option for you right away. Volunteering to show off your spacious,

five-bedroom, five-thousand-square-foot mansion is highly competitive, and you'll probably end up on a long waiting list.

2) **Nursery duty**—Babies and toddlers need good loving arms to hold them while their parents are being preached at. It's safe to say that as long as you're *not* Michael Jackson or R. Kelly (most churches aren't as strict as the one I encountered), you'll be allowed to lend your services in the nursery. So don't be shy—guys, this means you too—get yourself some anti-germ baby wipes, take your vitamin C, learn to hold your breath for long periods of time, and volunteer in the nursery.

3) **Ushering**—Once a job allotted for old white men with bad cologne, today's ushers feature savvy fashion statements, infectious smiles, and well-mannered welcoming statements. Let's face it, you don't have to be the brightest person on the planet to hand out bulletins and pass the offering plate, so this volunteer opportunity is for the person who is looking for an easy high-profile job with little-to-no overstraining commitment.

4) **Teaching children's Sunday school**—Although you do have to have a passion for felt board, puppets, and "I-think-I-know-more-about-Moses-than-you" seven-year-old brats, this job is a breeze. Most churches supply all necessary teaching tools, such as Bible stories, examples, and arts and craft supplies—add in your own creative

measure of what to serve for snack, and you have yourself a Sunday school class fit for the finest of students. One downside to teaching Sunday school is the songs that tend to be popular. You may want to go to your local Christian bookstore and find a CD that will teach you "My God Is So Big" and "This Little Light of Mine"—and yes, you HAVE to do the motions!

5) **A singer in the praise and worship band**—Get your vocal-prowess ready, practice singing your best "do, ray, me," and be prepared for some serious competition. Gone are the days of just anyone "making a joyful noise" in church with a microphone in their hands. Many of today's church praise and worship bands have serious talent. Although you'll probably have to start the process by singing in the church choir, wearing one of those funny looking robes, and volunteering for at least one Easter pageant, have no fear, you'll eventually work your way up to the front of the stage and stand alongside a man holding a green Epiphone guitar and be asked to emotionally involve yourself in every song for 8:00, 9:30, and 11:00 services. You may also want to work out your arms—raising your hands for long periods of time will be expected!

6) **Janitorial responsibilities**—Although you'll rarely get mentioned from the pulpit for your great pew cleaning skills, this volunteer opportunity has its hidden advantages. Usually, the cleaning gets done after church hours, when

there is no one else in the church, so making use of
those impressive open-church building acoustics is a blast.
Singing, whistling, and pretending you're Tom Brokaw
from *NBC Nightly News* is extremely enhanced with that
built-in reverb that only a church building can offer. Sure,
you're vacuuming, dusting, and cleaning out other people's
poop stains from toilets, but the chance to raise your voice
at the top of your lungs and hear it all around you is
worth every bit of that disgusting volunteer work. Besides,
you can also check out what's inside your pastor's top
office drawer—that's always invigorating.

7) **Leading an adult small group**—If you're even
beginning to think about this, you deserve some extreme
props. When done right, leading adult small groups is
highly rewarding, but also emotionally, spiritually, and
physically exhausting. Lots of prep time goes into helping a
group of ten couples come closer to the God, so before
you venture off and do something drastic for Jesus, make
sure you're well aware that membership may have its
privileges, but also its quirks!

8) **Special music**—Although in some churches, special
music is a lost art, it's still a great way to utilize your
singing and instrument talent in front of a larger audience.
Keep in mind though, those of us who *think* we're
talented, yet can't sing or play our way out of a paper
bag should refrain from volunteering in this area. There
is nothing worse than sitting through a soloist attempting

to hit out-of-reach notes with a pitch-less voice, all the while trying to acknowledge God's glory throughout—it just ain't cool. Situations like this are unnecessary struggling moments for the cynics and jokesters in your church body—remember, it's never cool to cause your brother to stumble. So be nice to your fellow God-lovers—if you can't sing—*don't!*

KEY VERSE TO REMEMBER

"Do not hide Your face from me, Do not turn Your servant away in anger; You have been my help; Do not abandon me nor forsake me, O God of my salvation." —Psalms 27:9

This is certainly not an exhaustive list of volunteer opportunities available for the newly churched or the "new-to-this-church" individual, but this will get you started. Remember though, volunteering is all about serving one another; it's about helping, and not about be being a pest. Refrain from over-saturating your welcome. When you volunteer, you want people to want you there. You certainly don't want to get yourself in a situation where the people you are helping are actually secretly wishing you had never volunteered. And this happens—a lot! Also, don't over-commit—that's always a bad thing. Involvement and community is the key to fitting into your new church body—so don't forget to volunteer!

OVER-WORKING
SS-THAN BEAUTIFUL REPUTATION OPPORTU
LOTS OF GRACE
REMEMBER ALL CHURCHES VARY
KNOW BEFORE
DON'T BE SURPRISED

A COUPLE OF TRUTHS TO KNOW BEFORE YOU VOLUNTEER... AT A CHURCH

➡   I'm not trying to be mean or condescending to my
       religious kind, but truth is, Christians are much more
       difficult to work with than most other sects of people.
       In fact, in a recent study citing the most-loved people in
       the world, evangelical Christians came in just above
       lesbians. So it's not surprising that we have a less-than-
       beautiful reputation when it comes to the way we deal
       with people. So don't be surprised if you're taken
       advantage of while volunteering at church. Most volunteer
       opportunities are over-working, non-paying gigs that
       require lots of grace on the part of the volunteer.

➡   In many churches, when it comes to volunteering, a little
       thing called *sexism* does apply. If you're thinking about
       "applying" for a job that is generally associated with your
       opposite sex, you may want to speak with the person in
       charge of the selection committee before you submit your
       name for duty. All churches vary in their assigned male and
       female church roles, so you'll need to do some snooping
       around to know what your church's acceptable gender
       norms happen to be.

MORE THAN JUST VOLUNTEERING

Church involvement is much more than just volunteering. There are certainly other ways to interact with the churched. From Sunday school classes to being a choir or orchestra member to attending small groups, most churches offer a wide variety of options where members are normally encouraged to participate.

In fact, churches have become quite savvy in their attempt to make extracurricular church activities work around today's Christian's busy schedule. For example, if you're unable to attend church on Sunday morning, there's a pretty good chance a church near you offers a Saturday night service. Also, many churches now offer "middle of the week" Bible classes for those who desire more spiritual content throughout their workweek. On top of Bible studies, some churches offer college and seminary courses, and also one-time seminars that discuss special theological topics. It's important to read through your church bulletin or ask one of your pastors what is offered at your particular church.

MULTI-CHURCHING

A new trend that was unheard of ten to twenty years ago is sweeping the nation: It's called multi-church involvement. I know several people who live in metropolitan areas and refuse to only be involved in one church. Churchgoers with such savoir-faire usually have a "home" church they attend on Sunday mornings, but when it comes to extracurricular activities, they choose from a smorgasbord of options from various churches in their area. Many of today's Christians are less worried about doctrine and theology and more interested in spiritual benefits.

FIVE BENEFITS TO MULTI-CHURCHING

1 **Options**—From service times to ministry opportunities to youth functions, multi-churching gives you options. Your schedule is much more flexible when you know that you have the option of catching a Sunday night service at three of your six church "homes."

2 **Faith differences**—No more arguing among family members about differences in personal faith preferences. If there's one in your family who prefers a charismatic twist to his or her worship, while you desire a more liturgical service, multi-churching solves this problem for both of you.

3 **Youth programs**—Many smaller churches do not have the financial capabilities to offer an aggressive youth program. Well, multi-churching allows you to send your child to any number of quality youth functions in your area.

4 **Teaching**—Various churches give one the opportunity to hear preachers with different viewpoints about Christianity. It's a good way to help develop your own opinions and compare them with others in the Christian faith.

5 **Relationships and community**—Probably the best

thing about multi-churching is the ability to meet all kinds of people and build relationships with Christians throughout your community.

CHURCH SMALL GROUPS

Many churches have gone the way of first century Christians by having each member become a part of a church-led small group. With many pastors of larger churches finding it difficult to effectively connect and interact with their members (heck, they can't even remember the names of half of their staff), they have found it necessary to establish house churches in different locations around the church's community to help fulfill the physical, emotional, and spiritual needs of its people.

If you're involved in a church that offers small groups, I highly recommend trying to attend. I'll be honest; they're not for everyone. Some people find it difficult to open up in small settings. But if the small group leader is a kind and compassionate leader who is good at including the entire group in discussion time, even those who are skeptical of small groups should find house churches a comfortable supplement to the Sunday morning church experience.

CHAPTER 5

THE WORSHIP
SERVICE

→ SEVEN CLICHÉS THAT NEED TO GO—NOW

→ FIVE IDEAS CHURCHES SHOULD TRY

→ HOW TO MAKE CHURCH MORE INTERESTING

THE WORSHIP SERVICE

Chapter 5

Even with the strides modern Christian culture has made in the last couple of decades to improve its reputation among mainstream society, churches still fight being stereotyped as stuffy, pretentious, and lacking in originality and vision.

Sadly, Christians seem to be afraid to venture out of their past *and* present religious routines. I believe we as a culture need to move toward a God-worship that utilizes both forward thinking and imagination. I've experienced more than my share of dead churches in my lifetime, churches that seem to stifle believers instead of setting us free. Much of my Christian life has been stifled and confined by my church experiences.

SEVEN CHURCH CLICHÉS THAT NEED TO GO—NOW

1 **Announcements in the middle of praise and worship music**—There is nothing more annoying than to be worshiping God in song one second and hearing about Tuesday night's senior potluck dinner the next. Either put all of the announcements in the church bulletin or don't mention them until after the service is over. I can't imagine Jesus stopping in the middle of His beatitudes and letting everyone know that Peter and John would be hosting a Saturday afternoon fish fry.

2 **Praise and worship flags**—Note to pastor or praise and worship leader: We don't like the pink, purple, and blue "Hosanna" flags—especially when they're carried and waved around during singing time. Let us do the praising; we don't need any loud-colored flags to do that for us.

3 **"Visitor" time**—Attention all churches: When you're visiting a church, the last thing you want to do is raise your hand and let the entire church know that you're visiting for the first time. We don't want to wear a nametag. And we don't want the pastor to come by and visit us. If you happen to be visiting a church and you've been "spotted" by an usher as a "first timer," try putting the little nametag they give on the end of your nose and see what they say.

4 **Praise and worship guitar solos**—Praise and worship is a time of one-on-one intimacy with God. We don't ever need to have an early-'90s-styled, power-guitar solo in the middle of "Lord, I Lift Your Name On High"—*ever.*

5 **Interpretive dancing**—I know David danced before the Lord—and I'm sure he was great—but fourteen-year-old wannabe ballerinas displaying their dance-recital moves to MercyMe's "I Can Only Imagine" during a church service is *always* awkward.

6 **Five-minute sermon prayers**—Usually it's the head deacon or elder who stands behind the pulpit and delivers the very long, drawn-out, prayerful pre-sermonette.

No matter who it is, people who pray church prayers that last longer than two minutes in length are probably bringing glory to themselves and not to God.

7 **Any mention of sports by the pastor**—Okay, I'll let pastors slide on the retelling of the story about the guy in *Chariots of Fire*, but that's it. All other sporting events and stories should be declared off limits. I know it makes you feel cool and relevant to talk about your love for a particular team, but no one cares that your team won or lost the day before. We don't want you to wear your team's jersey on Sunday mornings, and to be honest, we've never thought you were really masculine enough to even like sports.

KEY VERSE TO REMEMBER

"God is spirit, and those who worship Him must worship in spirit and truth." John 4:24

The stereotypes of the church being stuffy and pretentious have crippled my ability to be my real self inside the walls of the church. To put it plainly, I was never able to laugh out loud when I saw or heard something funny in church.

One Sunday morning as a seventeen-year-old sitting in the church's third row from the front, I listened to the lady at the piano sing a solo. The church had only just started; the assistant pastor hadn't even welcomed the visitors yet. To be honest, I was steeling myself to try to stay awake through a long morning.

About halfway through the soloist's sour rendition of "He Touched Me," a very large lady with thick, black-rimmed glasses got out of the pew two rows behind me and proceeded to walk up the aisle. A determined look on her face and resolution in her heavy step, she was heading straight up to the platform where the pastors and the choir were sitting. I had never seen such a thing in all my church-visiting years. This lady looked as though she were on a serious mission from God Himself.

The entire church, the choir, and the pastor himself were staring at her in utter befuddlement. Completely unconcerned, she walked straight up to the pastor, leaned over, and began to whisper in his ear.

This motion prompted a collective gasp from the congregation and suppressed hysterical laughter from the choir—for good reason: The lady was practically mooning us. At least half of Mrs. Skeyler's large bum was peeking out of her bright pink sweatpants as she leaned over to reach the pastor's ear. Pastor's face went bright red; he clearly had no idea what to do.

But once she'd finished whatever she wanted to say, Mrs. Skeyler hiked her pants back up and walked calmly back to her seat as if it were the most ordinary thing in the world. The congregation took a collective breath of relief, and the service continued almost uninterrupted.

I started laughing hysterically. It was funny. It's not every Sunday that you see a lady's large behind staring back at you from the church platform. The pastor looked at me sharply, and I quickly lowered my laughter to a wavering snicker. I learned quickly that mixing church with laughter was often not welcomed—especially, when it was disrupting a part of the service.

Needless to say, I ended up looking like a buffoon.

I feel that an important part of any God-worship experience is the freedom to truly be *you*. And sadly, in many of today's churches, individuals can't be themselves. I think it's important to feel comfortable in a church service. Sadly, many times the preconceived notion of church is that of a formal experience; often times individual personalities get minimized in the worship process, so most churches end up "bringing on" a very homogenous encounter with God.

However, God is not a homogenous being. How could He be? He is the author of everything creative. Let's face it, I could sit here and write some cheesy paragraph about Him being the creator of all the colors of the rainbow and the birds of the air, but I'm not going to do that. If you can't look outside the window of your house into the blue sky and see that God is creative, then there is something sincerely wrong with you. Nothing I write in this book is going to change your mind. Sadly, despite the inescapable truth of God's artistic nature, we as His followers often find it difficult to celebrate His majesty with imagination.

FIVE STUPID YET IMAGINATIVE IDEAS CHURCHES SHOULD TRY
(YOU TOO CAN MAKE CHURCH MORE INTERESTING!)

1 Churches should start having rhythmic gymnastics presented in the aisles of the church. The little hoops, balls, and "string on a sticks" would go nicely with the already purchased worship flags.

2 Pastors should enter from the rear of the church auditorium proceeded by bagpipes, "Jesus" floats, and a horn section.

3 Public displays of pastoral council should become a regular part of the service. Can you imagine? Instead of hearing all the gossip a couple of days later from the pastor's wife, you'll be privy to all of the problems of your most-dear friends every single Sunday morning, *plus* you'll also hear the good advice your pastor offers—it would be better than reality TV. Heck, I'll volunteer to be the guinea pig on the first Sunday.

4 Churches should have wireless Internet capability. Churchgoers everywhere could bring their laptops with them to church and check out Foxnews.com, ESPN.com or, umm ... use Crosswalk.com's Bible study tools to enhance the pleasure and the strategic impact of the pastor's sermon.

5   Instead of doughnuts and coffee on Sunday mornings, think pancakes, bacon, and scrambled eggs.

However, in all seriousness, God-worship should be passionate and engaging. I've experienced this kind of worship publicly, in a community setting, only a few times in my life, but every time it happens, I am left utterly changed by meeting God face-to-face. Sure, sometimes it's with fascinating music, spoken word, drama, and art that I experience God. Yet it doesn't necessarily have to be a cutting edge, "shock and awe" experience to be engaging. Many times simplicity is a lost art in today's churches. We've become more about the bells and whistles in our services than we are about connecting man with a powerful, awesome God. We need to stop trying to show the Church what worshiping God is about, and find new ways to invite them along for the ride—to become a part of it. I don't have all the answers. By now, you can certainly see that. But I'm hoping that churches all over the world will read this crazy book and begin thinking outside the plain, old, ordinary box, and try new things. God is among us. He doesn't have to be "ushered" in. He said, where two or more are gathered together, He is there. So whether we're at the grocery store, the gym, or the church— worship should be happening.

GETTING ALONG
WITH CHRISTIANS

→ FIVE HIGHLY OFFENSIVE PHRASES

→ FIVE THINGS I'VE LEARNED ABOUT CHRISTIANS

→ THREE RESPONSES TO THE HOLY SPIRIT DEFENSE

GETTING ALONG WITH CHRISTIANS

Chapter 6

As I stated in one of the lists from a previous chapter, Christians can sometimes be hard to get along with. No wonder Christian bookstores have countless titles on building healthy relationships with others, faith survival, and not letting jerks get the best of you. It's a jungle out there in the church world. I have certainly encountered my share of weird, mean Christians in my lifetime.

Back in 1992, when I was eighteen, I was walking into the church with my boom box one Sunday morning. As always, an usher and a deacon waited at the front door to greet me. But instead of his usual friendly "good morning," the deacon took me aside and whispered in my ear, "How many *niggers* did you have to tackle to get that there CD player?"

I was appalled. I looked at him in shock.

"What?" he asked me. "Don't tell me you're offended by a little *nigger* joke."

I didn't have the courage to say anything to him. I just smiled and walked away.

In the church I was attending then, this kind of behavior was common. Maybe conservative churches tend to attract the type of Christians who just enjoy saying really stupid things. Or maybe they really don't know any better. But I hate the way the idiotic few make a bad name for the rest of us.

FIVE PHRASES HIGHLY OFFENSIVE TO MANY CHRISTIANS
(YOU MAY WANT TO AVOID SITUATIONS WHERE THESE PHRASES MAY BE USED.)

1 **"You're sexy!"** Some people truly believe that Christians aren't allowed to be sexy. I've used this phrase on several occasions and have offended many in the process.

2 **"I'm a democrat."** Most Christians assume *all* Christians are right-winged lovers of George W. Bush. I've heard several arguments break out after one of the faithful few came out of the closet as a liberal-minded Clinton fan.

3 **"Would you like to see a wine list?"** Have you ever been to dinner with a Christian who was quite vocal on how drinking alcohol was not on their to-do list? Well, when I'm with that particular friend of mine, I always shiver when a server comes over to the table to recommend a wine or beer to go with dinner. My dry, always-sober friend can never just say "no, thank you." He always has to pull out the "I'm proud to have never tasted alcohol" speech.

4 **"I don't think there's anything wrong with being gay!"** I think small spiritual wars have been started over such a statement.

5   **"How do you know that God is indeed a man?"** When you hear these words, just run, because there's about to be an explosion of words. DO NOT UNDER ANY CIRCUMSTANCES MAKE YOUR "GOD IS A FEMALE" OPINION KNOWN TO THE MASSES. You'll get hurt.

Oh, but I've met many idiots over the years. When I was the editor of *CCM* magazine, the largest Christian music magazine in the world, we ran a feature on Latin Christian singer Jaci Velasquez with a heading that read, "Crazy! Sexy? Christian." Many of the regular readers were infuriated by this title. They responded with emails, letters, and phone calls. And as the editor, it was my job to talk to all the angry subscribers who called in.

"Hello, this is Matthew," I answered one such call in as friendly a tone as I could muster. Sometimes friendliness defuses an antagonist's irritation. "Can I help you?"

"I don't know if you can help me or not," snapped a Michigan lady whose tone certainly proved my friendliness theory wrong. But at least she got straight to her point. "I am outraged," she told me angrily, "that you would use the word *sexy* to describe Jaci Velasquez." Her voice rose shrilly. "MY FIFTEEN-YEAR-OLD BOY READS YOUR MAGAZINE!"

"Well ma'am," I replied placatingly, "we're not actually calling Jaci sexy in the article. If you'll look, you'll see a question mark at the end of the …"

"I DON'T CARE IF THERE'S A QUESTION MARK!" she interrupted me sharply. "WHY WOULD A CHRISTIAN MAGAZINE USE THE WORD SEXY?"

"Ma'am, we were only attempting to communicate a criticism that many of Jaci's fans have voiced to her."

"I DON'T WANT MY BOY SEEING THE WORD SEXY IN A CHRISTIAN MAGAZINE," she screamed. "THEY DON'T HEAR THE WORD SEXY AT MY HOUSE. I EXPECTED MORE FROM YOU. DO YOU PEOPLE READ YOUR BIBLE?"

I was taken aback. "Yes, ma'am, of course we do."

"WELL, YOU CAN'T TELL! BECAUSE SEX IS NOT IN THE BIBLE!"

"Um …" At this point I started to lose patience. "Actually, it is."

"NO, it is NOT!" she insisted.

"Ma'am," I retorted, my temper snapping, "Sex is talked about throughout the Bible."

"ARE YOU CONTRADICTING ME, YOUNG MAN?" the woman shouted into the telephone. "THE WORD SEX IS NOT USED IN THE BIBLE!"

"Yes it IS!" By now my tone was rising too, and I hit the speakerphone so my colleagues could listen in (and laugh).

"NOT IN THE KING JAMES VERSION, IT ISN'T!" The lady's voice was now echoing through the office. "SEX IS TO BE A TOPIC THAT IS DISCUSSED BETWEEN A MAN AND A WOMAN IN THE PRIVACY OF THEIR BEDROOM! IT IS ORDAINED BY GOD AND NOT BY YOU, YOUNG MAN! CANCEL MY SUBSCRIPTION!" And she hung up.

How do you talk to someone like this? It was fine for her to disagree with our use of the word "sexy." I thought it was a little strange that she didn't want her fifteen-year-old son to even hear the word, but that's her prerogative. She has a right to her opinion. But why can't she at least discuss it in a normal manner?

In Christian culture, it seems, normal has an entirely different definition.

FIVE THINGS I HAVE LEARNED ABOUT CHRISTIANS

1 When you think you're going to offend someone, you probably are. That doesn't mean that you stop what you're doing—just be prepared for the repercussions.

2 Criticism is rarely welcomed in a church setting. You can be as nice as possible, but you'll be "criticized" behind your back for constructive feedback of almost any kind. (Editor's note: This rule does not apply if you're James Dobson or Rick Warren.)

3 Christians tend to make judgments first, and think about stuff second.

4 Most Christians have very little sense of humor; even when they "get" the joke and know that you were kidding—they will not laugh.

5 For the majority of people, you're never supposed bring up religion or politics, but a Christian's politics is his religion (and vice versa).

$\mathbf{B}$eing the editor of *CCM* magazine gave me the opportunity to meet many of the strange and intriguing individuals who make their home inside the bubble of Christian culture. The magazine's readers were often shockingly otherworldly, but by far the most interesting people I met were the independent Christian musicians who sought out my advice regarding their musical careers. One of my favorite individuals was a singer/songwriter named Susan.

Susan was a guitar player and a singer who had recently formed a band to perform the songs she'd written. When she recruited me to give her my professional opinion regarding her musical talents, she and I met up at a local coffeehouse for a brainstorming session. She brought her demo CD and a portable CD player; I brought my ears and my expertise.

As I sat down at the small table with my extra-shot mocha frappacino, Susan asked if she could pray before starting our meeting. "Of course," I said, expecting one of those brief formulaic prayers that Christians sometimes use before meetings, similar to saying grace. But I was mistaken. Ten minutes and about a hundred "praise you, Jesus, for Matthew's willingness to listen to these songs!" later, I was wishing I'd bypassed the whole prayer thing. It was getting embarrassing, hearing her thank God for me repeatedly … especially since I hadn't done anything yet.

People who over-spiritualize everything tend to freak me out.

Still, I tried to keep an open mind as we began listening to her first song. In a situation like that, I don't usually expect the music, lyrics, or vocals to be up to par with a Nashville-produced record. But when someone tells me they're pursuing a career in music, I don't anticipate a raucous cacophony when I'm listening to their demo CD. And that's exactly what I heard as track number one kicked off. The vocals were off-key and nasal. The guitar was utterly simplistic, something like what a ten-year-old would play in his first week of music lessons. And the song was horrible—*really* horrible.

My first and most honest thought was that Susan needed to immediately get in her car, drive back to Jefferson City, Mo., and get a job at Wal-Mart, because if this demo was any indication of her talent, Susan was never going to make it in music.

But of course, I couldn't say that!

My next inclination was to burst into laughter. But I couldn't do that either. So instead I sat there calmly, trying to think of one good thing to say about her music.

As I stared out the window of the coffeehouse, trying not to laugh and avoiding Susan's eyes, my attention was pulled back by a movement across the table. Susan bopping her head to the beat, grinning from ear to ear and fervently mouthing the words to her own song. A plump woman in her late twenties with big '80s hair, it struck me that even if she were a great musician, Susan hardly had the look to command a powerful stage presence. And in the entertainment industry, appearance always matters—even in the Christian music industry.

The song finally ground to a halt. Susan came back to earth and gazed at me anxiously, eagerly awaiting my verdict. I heard her murmuring softly under her breath; I think she was speaking in tongues.

"Susan," I began awkwardly, "first of all, I want you to know that I am only one person with one opinion." I forced a grin. "Other people in this town might say something completely different."

"Oh, I know all about that," Susan replied, laughing and looking somewhat relieved. "Everybody has their opinions."

"Well," I tiptoed over my words as gingerly as I could, feeling even more hesitant as I saw her impatience. "I don't want this to sound harsh, but in my opinion, that song needs a lot of work."

In an instant, her face fell from elation to distress.

"Your vocals are flat in areas," I continued, gaining strength with honesty. "And I think the lyrics could use some reworking."

"I don't want to change that song," retorted Susan with an offended look. "The Holy Spirit gave me that song. It's not mine to change; He *entrusted* it to me."

I looked at her quizzically. "You wrote this song, right?" I asked.

"Well," she hesitated. "Yes and no."

"Yes and no? What do you mean?"

"Well, I wrote it down," she admitted reluctantly, "but that song was a gift from the Holy Spirit. I don't feel comfortable claiming that song as mine."

Well, I agreed with her there. I wouldn't have felt comfortable claiming that song as mine, either.

But Susan was glaring at me with growing dislike. "I just don't understand how you can criticize a song that is *obviously* Holy Spirit inspired," she told me.

I guess it was then that I lost patience. "Well," I retorted briskly, "if the Holy Spirit indeed wrote that song, then something horrible happened to it during the transition from his hands to yours." I smiled brightly. "So—do you want me to listen to the next song?"

THREE RESPONSES WHEN SOMEONE USES THE HOLY SPIRIT DEFENSE

1 "That used to be the Holy Spirit's? Wow! (Wait two seconds.) It's been in your possession for quite some time, huh?"

2 "*You*, my friend, are completely full of crap."

3 "Aw, I never knew the Holy Spirit did cross stitch." (Turn the work of "art" over and quickly say: "Oh gosh, He needs to work on his backstitching!")

Perhaps, you haven't had any bad run-ins with Christians. But no doubt, you will! It's inevitable. One of these days, you will be utterly sideswiped by the actions of an individual who claims to know and love Jesus. Believe me, it hurts. And it never gets much easier. Sadly, there's very little you can do to prepare for such an encounter. My best advice is to say as little as possible during the interaction. Silence usually diffuses even the most horrific of situations.

BOYCOTTS
AND EXTREMES

→ THREE TYPES OF EXTREMISTS TO LOOK OUT FOR

→ TODAY'S MOST POPULAR ONGOING BOYCOTTS

→ A LITTLE LEARNED ADVICE

→ THREE SIGNS YOU'RE ABOUT TO DO SOMETHING STUPID

BOYCOTTS AND EXTREMES

BOYCOTTS AND EXTREMES

Chapter 7

Christians love to boycott. We will boycott at the drop of a hat. Give us a cause to hate, and we'll make sure that every Christian from Kansas City to Bangkok knows about the boycott. And we'll do our dead-level best to get every God-fearing fanatic to join in our evangelical embargo. Somewhere between finding Jesus and proclaiming Him as our Savior, boycotting must become a part of our nature.

Often, the severity of the cause doesn't really matter. Christians will boycott for almost any petty grievance. Do you think Barbie is showing too much cleavage? Call your neighborhood Christian, and I'm sure he'd be glad to start an email campaign against the toy icon. Do you have an openly gay couple living in your community? We'll have picketers and protesters there in a heartbeat. Is your employer preventing you from wearing your "Jesus Is the Reason for the Season" holiday pin? Don't worry—we've got lawyers and government officials to handle your case for you. We'll even turn the campaign into a popular Christian radio show and call it ministry. All it takes is a couple of phone calls.

As a child, I went through an unending series of boycotts. We took them very seriously; violating a boycott was just one step down from heresy. But they never lasted long. Usually, within a few weeks or months, we'd forget them in favor of the next up-and-coming Christian cause.

A LIST OF TODAY'S MOST POPULAR ONGOING BOYCOTTS

1) **All things Disney**—Mickey, Donald, and gang are like Satan's toys in some Christians' minds. Ever since Michael Eisner created "gay" day at Walt Disney World, Christians have been up in arms over the entertainment company. Although, at least Disney is an equal opportunity kind of place—they also sponsor a weekend for Christians every September.

2) **Halloween**—Rumored to be a night when witches and warlocks are up to no good, many Christians skip out on candy corn and dressing up to "celebrate" Satan Day. Although, some churches have started sponsoring their own Christian harvest night. Kids dress up like Bible characters and eat candy corn.

3) **Madonna, Britney, Christina, and Janet**—Music's biggest female artists are also some of Christianity's greatest foes.

4) **"R" Rated Movies**—Not many Christians will publicly admit to viewing rated R movies. However, we also have a hard time admitting we struggle reading the Bible and praying sometimes.

5) **All Things Mormon**—Note: This does not include trampolines and the Mormon Tabernacle Choir.

6)   **Budweiser, Miller, and Coors**—God forbid if one of these companies is sponsoring a concert you want to go see. Many Christians boycott events where leading beer companies are associated—but for some reason, this rule never applies to sporting events.

MY PERSONAL BOYCOTTING

My father came home from work one afternoon and showed the entire family a photocopied picture of a half-moon with a warning label on it. The moon had a nose, some eyes, and a mouth, and it seemed to be leering at me shiftily from the fuzzy picture.

"This moon," Dad said gravely, "is a cult icon."

"What's a cult?" asked my sister blankly.

"It's a group of supposedly religious people who are *really* enemies of God," my Mom said, looking very seriously at my eight-year-old sister and clearly making a mental note about further instruction on the enemies of God.

I felt my heart beat faster. I had a subconscious mental picture of the "enemies of God" lurking around every tree, ready to pounce on me, force me to deny my faith, and then maybe send me to the guillotine. Any mention of them always sent my pulse racing.

Dad continued his grim announcement. "I'm afraid that a few of the products we use every day are financially supporting the Church of Satan."

"The *Church* of *Satan?*" Mom gasped, horrified. *We*, a God-fearing, fundamentalist, Bible-believing family, were somehow unconsciously supporting the most terrible spiritual enemy in the universe?

"I just got this official notice from a fundamentalist friend at work," Dad continued, overriding her yelp of protest. "It says that a company by the name of Procter & Gamble, which sells several household products, is using its profits to support Satan and his causes."

"How do we know which products are Procter and Gamble?" Mom demanded, recovering quickly from the shock and rallying with a determined glint in her eye.

Dad hesitated, turning the picture over in his hands. "Well," he said, "it's my understanding that we should get rid of all the products that have this moon icon here on the packaging."

Mom turned without a word and stalked into the kitchen, resolve written on her every feature. Not one more cent of *her* money was going to the Church of Satan—that was for darn sure.

I got the job of going through all the cupboards, cabinets, shelves, and closets, searching for the little faced moon. As it turned out, the moon products were all of my mom's favorites. But Dad was insistent, and every PG product went straight to the big trashcan out back.

I threw away a box of Tide, a bottle of Ivory liquid, a roll of Bounty paper towels, six rolls of Charmin bathroom tissue, a jug of Mr. Clean, three tubes of Crest toothpaste, Mom's Secret deodorant, a canister of Folgers coffee, a bottle of Sunny Delight, and a can of Pringles. Pretty much all of the high-quality products in the house were trashed. And with every item I tossed, I could almost see those lurking enemies of God retreating.

But as Mom realized exactly which products Procter & Gamble

manufactured, her determination went downhill. In fact, by now she was a little bewildered.

"Virgil, do we really have to throw out the Bounty paper towels?" she asked, glancing at my dad pleadingly. In retrospect, I really think she had a point. Let's face it: Bounty paper towels are the best. And how much of the $1.59 a roll was actually being donated to Satan? Three cents? But my father was adamant; everything had to go.

For a while, Mom religiously abstained from purchasing any of PG's well-advertised, top-of-the-line products. And since it's never fun to boycott alone, Mom made sure all of our friends knew about the Satanic products too. But eventually, the little half-moon dude showed up in our house again.

Mom told me she just wasn't pleased with the store-brand products. "They may promise dependability," she said briskly, "but they're simply not as good as the devil-supporting products."

As it turned out, Dad quickly became skeptical of the PG boycott as well. Somebody at our church said the whole thing was a farce. So after about six weeks, the entire family went back to using the products we loved. I never did find out if it was true that Proctor & Gamble supported Satan. But at three cents to the dollar, I figure it was worth it.

A LITTLE LEARNED ADVICE ABOUT BOYCOTTING

➡ Boycotts hardly ever work.

➡ Publicized boycotts make Christians seem ridiculous and petty.

➡ If you decide to take the plunge and boycott something: be consistent.

➡ Don't EVER boycott something just because someone else is doing it. You almost always lose.

➡ Don't boycott anything without knowing the facts first.

One of the most publicized Christian boycotts in recent history was the entire Southern Baptist Convention's war against Disney for its stance on homosexuality. Disney wasn't at all fazed by the denomination's PR attacks. Why? Because Christian boycotts usually involve a lot more talk than action. In 1998, I spoke with the leader of a Washington D.C. Christian mother's organization. She was organizing an event publicizing the evil, worldly activities at Disney. But after telling me all about the event, she leaned and whispered into my ear, "Keep this between you and me, but I'm actually taking my family to Disney World in three weeks." I grinned at her—I found the irony hilarious. But it's actually ridiculous; why would someone subject others to a cause that they themselves don't believe in?

Partly because of that kind of hypocrisy, Christian boycotts generally do little more than publicize the very problem they're aimed against. Nearly every church in America protested the 1980s movie *The Last Temptation of Christ*. And that protest, in itself, was probably a good idea. A movie depicting Christ as a sinner is a mockery of all we believe in. But we actually brought a great deal of publicity and awareness to that low-budget film. *Temptation* would have probably gone unnoticed on the pop cultural radar screen apart from the publicity lent it by the protests. When Christians angrily rallied against it, nearly every news outlet in the country covered not the film, but the controversy—free publicity for Universal—and everybody wants to see the film everyone's talking about.

I decided soon after the failed attempt of the Southern Baptist Church to bring Disney to its knees that my days of Christian boycotting were over.

EXTREMES

I've always loved music. But most of the churches I visited taught that music—like so many other things—was, for the most part, worldly, secular, and evil. In one particular church, rock 'n' roll was the probably the third most popular topic for sermons, right behind hell and premarital sex.

RECORD BURNINGS

At least once a year, my church would sponsor a chapel service to talk about the dangers of rock 'n' roll music and the worldliness of the artists who make it. A "secular music specialist," who had spent hours dissecting the music, lyrics, lifestyle, and imagery of rock 'n' rollers, would come to the church and try to convince us to burn all our secular tapes and records and listen only to hymns.

Patch "the Jesus Pirate" was this church's favorite secular music guru. He started wearing a patch after his left eye was removed with cancer. A few kids in his church started calling him Patch, and the name stuck. After that, he began traveling around to churches presenting a program in which he portrayed a pirate, which was particularly cool since the patch was actually real. Eventually he became one of the premiere children's entertainers for our entire denomination.

THREE SIGNS THAT YOU'RE GETTING READY TO DO SOMETHING <u>STUPID</u>

1 **If you're doing it because everyone else is doing it**—No matter what it is you're contemplating, if you're thinking about doing it based on someone else doing, you're doing it for *all* the wrong reasons.

2 **If you're doing it based on an emotional reaction**—Emotions will fool you every time. What you're contemplating may very well be a good decision, but if it's a good decision today, it will be a good decision tomorrow as well. Make sure your mental and spiritual logic has fully kicked in before you make a rash decision.

3 **If you're doing it to make someone else happy**—Many of us have this over-powering desire to please others. In some cases, it's a beautiful quality, but it can also be dangerous when you feel unable to say "no" to someone or something. Never let outside opinions make the decision for you. It's fine to seek advice, but after that advice, go make your own decision. Let your "yes" be yes and your "no" be no.

One Sunday night, Patch "the Jesus Pirate" came to speak to the entire church about the dangers of secular music. He brought pictures, audio samples, video clips, and magazine interviews to (Aaarrh!) prove his point.

During Patch's two-hour presentation, he showed us pictures of KISS and told us that the band's acronym meant, "Knights In Satan's Service." He changed the words to Joan Jett's hit "I Love Rock 'n' Roll" to, *I hate rock 'n' roll, don't put a nickel in the jukebox, sinner!* All of my friends and I would walk around school singing this little tune.

Everyone in the church gasped collectively when Patch told us how shock metal rocker Ozzy Osbourne had bitten the head off a live bat. Whitney Houston's aunt was a psychic lover. Michael Jackson and Prince were both Jehovah's Witnesses. Madonna was just a fornicating heretic who was also—almost as bad—a fallen Catholic. The Eagles' "Hotel California" was all about the love of marijuana. And if you played rock music at loud decibels for long periods of time, it would kill all your houseplants.

But the pirate was just getting started. His criticism of worldly rock musicians was just the warm-up for accusations against supposedly Christian artists. Patch reveled in telling us that Amy Grant, in an interview with *Rolling Stone*, had admitted to having been "horny" once.

THREE TYPES OF EXTREMISTS TO LOOK OUT FOR IN CHRISTIAN CULTURE

1 **The Over-Zealous Regulator**—The O.Z. Regulator is the man or woman who has been SELF-appointed to be the church watchdog. No matter who it is, they have no qualms about approaching an individual regarding their need to make life changes.

2 **The Conspiracy Theorist**—This individual turns the smallest piece of news into a Satan-influenced scheme. Usually an avid fan of politics and world culture, the Conspiracy Theorist is constantly monopolizing the time of others attempting to prove their speculations true. Y2K is a great example. I knew many Christians who bought generators and stockpiled canned foods, and some even put in personal home base gas tanks in case of catastrophe.

3 **The Theological Thumper**—These people are insane biblical scholars. Attempting to relate everything that happens in life to a Bible verse or teaching, they end up disproving themselves with their tired arguments and theories. Many times this type of extremist ends up leaving the faith altogether.

Patch resisted the urge to play one of Amy Grant's songs. He said it was too rocky for church. He did play and violently denounce the music of Sandi Patty, Steve Green, Twila Paris, and Michael W. Smith. (For those of you who have no idea who any of these artists are, all four were staples of Christian music in the '80s. Sandi Patty was sort of a Mary Poppins meets Barbara Mandrell meets Jimmy Swaggert. Steve Green was Pavarotti meets Barry Manilow.) But to Patch, it didn't matter if the music was from Dolly, Bruce, Stryper, The Cure, Boy George, Madonna, or Amy Grant— he told us unequivocally that we should burn it all!

However, I always enjoyed a good Baptist "burn the abominating music" bonfire. It was Christian entertainment at its best! Many of the church members would come and watch the festivities. Usually our youth pastor would emcee the bonfire. The night's entertainment would kick off with a prayer:

"Dear Holy God, these kids have come here to burn their wretched rock 'n' roll music. They have made a hard decision to turn away from their rebellion and repent of their unholiness. Lord Jesus, as we burn these tapes and records, may You burn the evil desires within these kids …"

Then all the teenagers—and sometimes new adult converts as well—who desired to repent of their ungodly listening habits would place their multi-thousand dollar record and tape collections in a pile on the ground. Wood and paper would already be laid out in preparation for the event. Usually, the youth pastor got the honor of pouring lighter fluid all over the pile of Beatles, Aerosmith, and Poison records. Then the climax: He'd light a match and dramatically drop it on the pile.

As soon as the first sparks of flames were visible, the entire audience would erupt into applause. Some would shout, "Praise Jesus!" Others would just stand quietly, weeping tears of joy over their sons' or daughters' choice to purge the evil from their lives. The pastor would hover in the back of the crowd, grinning from ear to ear. The following Sunday, he would announce the names of all those who had burned their worldly music at the bonfire. "You young people who are still listening to that godless music should follow the example of these fine teens," he would conclude.

That church became consumed with proclaiming the evils of rock music, whether Christian or not, and we went to great lengths to avoid even the slightest association with anything resembling rock. When "pop/rock" beats were discovered in the church organ's rhythm memory, the organ was banned from use. When the 1988 graduating class from the church's Christian school wanted to use Michael W. Smith's song "Friends" as its theme song, it was refused.

The first "pop" song I remember hearing on the local Top 40 radio station was "Straight Up" by Paula Abdul. I thought it was heavenly. If anyone had told me then how much my attitudes about music were destined to change in the next ten years, well, I'd never have believed them.

CHAPTER 8

THE **DATING**

AND SEX CHAPTER

(PG-13)

→ SEVEN TYPES OF GUYS IN CHRISTIAN CULTURE

→ THE LINE BEFORE YOU'RE MARRIED

→ EIGHT TYPES OF GIRLS IN CHRISTIAN CULTURE

→ THREE TYPES OF INAPPROPRIATE CLOTHING IN CHRISTIAN CULTURE

→ THE FIVE TYPES OF COUPLES TO LOOK OUT FOR

THE DATING AND SEX CHAPTER(PG-13)
Chapter 8

I've sometimes thought that the Church had a vendetta against dating. Have you ever walked into a Christian bookstore for some "Christian" advice on dating? Shelf after shelf features books on everything from "dating God's way" to "kissing dating goodbye." But despite a new movement toward "group dates" and "courting," people have yet to stop pursuing relationships with the opposite sex. And since it's a God-given instinct to marry, and dating is the most common method for pursuing that, the Church probably isn't going to change it anytime soon.

But Christians insist on complicating the dating process. Do you want to know how many times I've gotten the "friend" talk from a girl because she suddenly decided that *Jesus* wanted to be her boyfriend? That is the worst approach to breaking up with someone that I have ever experienced. When the second girl in a row used this excuse with me, I looked at her and inquired, "When did you and Jesus have a DTR? Because the last I heard, He was still dating my last girlfriend."

SEVEN TYPES OF GUYS (FOR GIRLS TO CHOOSE FROM) IN CHRISTIAN CULTURE

1   **The Jesus Jock**—This young man is instantly recognizable by his involvement in everything that's Christian. From FCA to Young Life to BSU, the Jesus

Jock is the unapproachable young steed who is nice to everybody, declared the ultimate prize by most girls, and would never lower himself to dating just anybody. His handsome good looks, kind smile, and incessant use of the phrase, "Praise God!" make this young man nauseatingly perfect.

2   **The Unattractive Nice Guy**—He's the guy you *want* to have as a best friend, but girls cringe at the thought of sharing a bed with him. Instead of girls giving him handshakes and hugs, this young man gets pats on the back and distant hellos. Sometimes appearing rather desperate, this "in love-with-the-Lord" backward fellow has a hard time relating in groups of more than three people. Having read his Bible completely through at least two times, the Unattractive Nice Guy is a spiritual brain worthy of everyone's attention.

3   **The "Do You Think …?" Guy**—There's always one guy in the church who has the annoyingly obvious feminine lisp, sings in every choir, hangs out with all of the awkward girls, and gets beat up at least once by somebody much bigger than him. Oh, and yeah, most people think he is gay or somewhat bi-curious. We don't find out the truth until years later when he'll either show up in church with his wife and three kids or wearing a skin-tight black shirt, bleached-blond hair, and an "oh gosh, the pastor's suit is just dreadful" look on his face.

4 **The Big Brother**—Everyone's favorite normal-looking young man is well-mannered and a decent student of the Bible. He's pretty much off-limits when it comes to dating because he has had a steady girlfriend since he was seventeen years old. He plans to be married after graduating from college.

5 **The Bad "Christian" Boy**—He's been going to church since he could pronounce the word "Jesus." Prone to trouble, his high school years were spent drugging and drinking it up. Because of his problem, he was kicked out of private school and sent to public school. Although he overcame his issue with addictions and returned to his faith, he never finished college, so he works for a construction company making ten dollars an hour. Not that there's anything wrong with that.

6 **The *My So-Called Life* Musical Guy**—His shoulder-length hair always seems to be on the verge of greasy as it constantly falls into his face. He pretends to love Mozart *and* Nirvana, and acts intellectual by asking the Sunday school teacher ridiculous questions that rarely make much sense. He usually has his own church harem of female "followers" who secretly want to date him, and there's always one guy who follows him around wanting to be *just* like him.

7 **The Extreme Guy**—He started skateboarding the same year he learned John 3:16. He's usually the first guy the youth pastor takes under his wing. Although he makes a decision for Jesus at almost every youth retreat or conference, his church attendance is frequently interrupted by snowboarding trips, late-night video game rallies, and rock climbing exhibitions. After graduating from college, God usually leads this young man into youth ministry. He ends up marrying an "I went to New York City and failed" supermodel and moving to some place like Utah or Nevada to work at a Christian camp.

EIGHT TYPES OF GIRLS (FOR GUYS TO CHOOSE FROM) IN CHRISTIAN CULTURE

1. **The Jesus Cheerleader**—Cute. Self-confident. Boisterous. The Jesus Cheerleader is the girl who's always first in line for Christian concert tickets, volunteer groups, and youth Bible studies. With a kick-butt smile and a perky personality, the J.C. female finds the good in just about everything. Although she's not necessarily the Bible whiz, her killer grin makes her the perfect candidate for the Sunday school teacher's pet. Often prone to kiss dating goodbye, the J.C. usually remains single until she meets the "big brother" man of her dreams while on a mission trip in Bolivia or Kenya.

2. **The Tomboy**—This young "sometimes masculine" woman is quiet and reserved. She prefers playing soccer over taking ballet, and she's usually the star pitcher on the

church-sponsored softball team. The Tomboy is usually the only girl strong enough or willing to brave the mosh pit at a P.O.D. or Skillet concert. Rarely one to date, she'll happily wrestle with you and is quite comfortable with you calling her by her last name.

3   **The Early Bloomer**—There's always one girl in youth group who has had "bosoms" since she was eight years old. As the young men's favorite girl until about 10th grade, this girl unfortunately ends up with the "I've kissed all of the cute guys in youth group" reputation. The Early Bloomer has a tendency to break down and cry in front of her girls' small group and confess her "physical" exploits. The room full of girls usually loves her back into the flock, but talks about her behind her back. She becomes bitter, leaves the church, marries a jerk, and usually doesn't return to her faith until her late-twenties.

4   **Miss Codependent**—Her parents have sheltered her from everything, including spiritual and emotional stability and healthy eating habits. Miss Codependent is the pimple faced girl who knows most of the answers to the Bible quiz questions, yet won't answer the question until she's asked to. Her quiet spirit, masqueraded as humility, usually becomes reliant and defined by her latest crush. Always prone to chase after the most popular guy in youth group, she becomes obsessed with calling his cell phone and emailing him. The worst "Miss Codependent" will eventually start falling asleep in church and "accidentally" whispering her current love's name—just for the attention.

5   **The Home School Girl**—She's the meek girl who is always carrying around a copy of *Great Expectations* or *Pilgrim's Progress*. She participates in ballet, gymnastics, karate, acting classes, chess tournaments, and piano recitals, and she rejects using make-up and dying her hair. Guys usually find this young lady intriguing and mysterious—when she's *not* wearing her thick glasses. Often not allowed to date until she turns 19, the Home School Girl usually decides for herself not to date until she's 22.

6   **The Sweet Innocent One**—She's the first one to say hello to you when you're the "new guy" in church. She's cute, bubbly, and a Bible champ. Every guy in youth group asks her out to "alternative" prom night, but she patiently waits to say "yes" until her ultimate vision of a man asks her out. She doesn't kiss on the third date, and second base is completely not in scheme of thinking. In college, the Sweet Innocent One joins the Christian sorority, where for the first time she meets girls who have drunk beer and had sex.

7   **"All About ME" Girl**—You will usually find the All About Me Girl heading up the praise band, making a dramatic display of lifted hands and desperate facial expressions. After asking how you are, she barely waits for an answer before launching into a passionate story about her trying week and the persecution she is enduring. All About Me Girl stars in all ministry promotional videos and usually ends up with a very quiet, introverted guy.

8   **The Premature Mother**—Often the quiet backbone of any church group, the Premature Mother is always the one to whip up the potato salad at any event, and you'll find her washing the dishes and sweeping out the church bus afterwards. She's the one to see about securing a Band-Aid or some Advil. Mature beyond her years, she intimidates the guys and usually ends up with someone about five to ten years her senior.

Another popular "Christian" way of breaking your significant other's heart is to tell him you feel God is asking you to take the next six months to "fast" from dating. In fairness, I have to admit that I've used this excuse myself. The problem is that you usually meet someone new a month later. Just in the last year, I have had several friends of mine announce that God wanted them to fast from dating. One is now married and the other is in a serious relationship, both to people they met during their time of fasting. So much for six months.

But we guys have our dating issues as well. In addition to the ubiquitous guy problem with commitment, Christian guys also have a problem that I like to call the "oh crap, I shouldn't have done that" syndrome. Consider this scenario: You meet a girl. You both like each other. You both desire purity in your relationship. And things start off great: You pray and read your Bibles together. But two weeks into the relationship, you somehow slip, and something happens that you think is too physical. Feeling guilty, you promise each other that it will never happen again. But after two weeks of spending more time praying and reading your Bibles, you do it again. And this time it's a little more intense, a little more serious. It's at this point that your girlfriend might pull the "Jesus wants to be my boyfriend" excuse and leave you. But if she doesn't do that, then you go home and become consumed with guilt. You decide, after more prayer and Bible reading, that the only thing you can do is break up with her. Except you somehow fail to mention to her that you want to break up! You just stop calling her. You don't return emails. You go on with life like she and that guilty moment never happened. She calls you. You let the voicemail pick it up. She calls you again. Voicemail. And after three days of her calling, you exasperatedly pick up the phone and call her back, acting surprised that she would call you so many times. "What's wrong?" she asks you, a dangerous tone in her voice.

"Oh nothing," you respond casually, "why do ask?"

Then she explodes. "Why haven't you called me in three days?!"

Does any of this sound familiar?

LET'S TALK ABOUT SEX

Almost as much as Christians are known for complicating dating, we are also well known for having long lists of taboos. Taboo lists vary significantly by location and church denomination. So you'll have to check with your local church authorities before creating your own personal list. However, sex and most anything related to sex is always on the list. Of course, despite popular opinion that we're a bunch of evangelical, Puritan-like prudes, Christians do *have* sex, but it's only allowed, encouraged, or talked about within the confines of a marriage relationship, between a man and woman. Any other sexual activity is sinful in the eyes of the churched. So if you're a new follower of Jesus Christ, and your past included sexual activity, you had better get yourself a chastity belt, because you're in for a bumpy, "frustrated" ride.

THAT'S IN THE BIBLE?

"As they were preparing to retire for the night, all the men of Sodom, young and old, came from all over the city and surrounded the house. They shouted to Lot, 'Where are the men who came to spend the night with you? Bring them out so we can have sex with them.'" —Genesis 4:11-12

Christians tend to be shy when talking about sex in public. We dance around the "act" like a five-year-old kid who's just learned how to say the word penis. However, all of the preachers I have ever heard speak on the topic of sex—and there are many—never mention the penis or the vagina. It's apparently been deemed inappropriate to say such words in a church setting. Well, we now live in a society where kids are learning descriptive sexual terms by the time they're six years old, and the church needs to respond accordingly.

DO IT LIKE A MISSIONARY

URBAN LEGEND OR NOT?

The missionary position got its name when the first European missionaries visited Africa. Native Africans had never seen a husband and a wife "do it" while the woman laid her back with the man facing her, his body positioned between her legs. The Africans called it the "missionary" position. And the name stuck.

Christian culture does have many *books* that describe the act of intercourse which are designed to teach young married evangelicals how to do more than the "missionary" position. These books have bad illustrations, quote long passages from Song of Solomon, and are written by people like James Dobson and Tim and Beverly LaHaye—the latter fact alone is enough to make someone a little nauseated.

When I was young, I would often look for these kinds of books in Christian bookstores. Christian sex books always intrigued me. Because I was never allowed to partake in "sex" conversations while at my church and Christian school, these very soft-pornesque Christian books gave me a little relief.

IF YOU'RE TRYING TO ABSTAIN FROM SEX—<u>DON'T EVER</u> ...

1) Trust yourself or the one who is with you ...
you *both* suck!

2) Leave it up to the other person to make the moral
decision... remember, you *both* suck!

3) Think that sex will *not* be a temptation. The desire will
swallow you up and *then* spit you out—but only if you
let it.

THE LINE BEFORE YOU'RE MARRIED:

HOW FAR IS TOO FAR?   THIS IS THE LINE...

I've heard many people ask their pastor or youth pastor this
question. And I've never heard a pastor give the same answer twice.
The same is true among the Christians I interviewed for this
particular list. I asked several Christian people this question (and got
many different answers):

WHAT ARE YOUR "PHYSICAL" BOUNDARIES IN A RELATIONSHIP?
HERE ARE A FEW OF THE ANSWERS:

1) "My girlfriend and I kiss, and make out, but that's about it—we both want to wait to have sex until we're married." —Leonard Woo, college student Harrisonburg, Virginia

2) "That's an embarrassing question. (laughs) Umm, I've seen my boyfriend naked before, but we haven't had sex, and won't." —Jennifer Krist, personal trainer, Des Moines, Iowa

3) "I've never kissed my boyfriend before. The first time I kiss him will be when we get married next May. And I can't wait." —Lillian Scott, college student, San Diego, California

4) "My girlfriend and I haven't had sex, but we've done pretty much everything else." —James Eberly, "tech guy," Chattanooga, Tennessee

5) "We only kiss. We're both virgins." —Melanie Wiltbanks, college student, Washington D.C.

6) "We set rules up at the beginning of our dating relationship. I'm not gonna lie; we've broken a couple of them, but for the most part, we've done pretty good. At least, I think so." —Daniel Trent, high school senior, Jefferson City, Tennessee

7)   "We have sex. We've *tried* not to, but it's too hard. We're
            engaged. I'm not sure if that makes a difference or
            not." —Kimberly Mitchell, first grade teacher,
            Philadelphia, Pennsylvania

VIRGINITY

In 1994 at a Christian music festival, I watched Christian
singer Rebecca St. James stand in front of 30,000 people—mostly
Christians—and proudly proclaim her vow of chastity until
marriage. The crowd erupted into thunderous applause. In our
enthusiasm, we rose to our feet to honor the young woman who is
arguably the world's third most popular virgin (right after the Virgin
Mary and Mother Theresa).

I joined in the cheering, shouting, and jumping up and down.
I was so excited about Rebecca's virginity—more excited than
I'd ever been about my own. No one had ever clapped for me,
but I was a virgin too. Actually, I'm pretty sure all of my friends
who came with me to the Christian festival that day were virgins.
None of us had ever received a standing ovation for our personal
chastity, but all of us stood there in that arena and eagerly gave it
up for Rebecca St. James. Well—let's not get carried away. We were
applauding, loudly. But I made a vow to God that day. I surrendered
my virginity over to my future wife. (I've made a few mistakes along
the way, but I've kept that vow … I'm getting married in October
2004.)

THREE TYPES OF VIRGINS

1. **Technical virgin**—A technical virgin has done "stuff"—including oral sex—that is sexually related, but has never had intercourse.

2. **Born-again virgin**—I'm not kidding. This is an actual term. A born-again virgin is an individual who has had sex before, but due to his recommitment to the Lord, his "spiritual" virginity has been given back to him.

3. **Physical virgin**—An individual who has never had any sexual contact with anyone else. And according to some Christian experts, this includes the act of masturbation.

MODESTY

When I was a teenager in the Christian school, modesty was almost as important as salvation. If something you were wearing caused your brother- or sister-in-Christ to stumble, the problem was quickly addressed. The girls undoubtedly had it the hardest. If a girl's skirt was too short, she was sent home. If her blouse was too low, she was sent home or made to safety pin the opening. If her shirt was too tight, the school provided her with a sweatshirt to wear over it for the rest of the day.

Guys could not wear shorts in front of women. We had to wear blue jeans or sweatpants for everything—even sports. To protect women from lusting after a man's hairy legs, the church made sure all males were properly and modestly clothed during any extracurricular activity. During the early years of my church experience, we were also not allowed to wear tanks or cutoff shirts. And armpit hair should *never* be visible. I mean, how can you expect a woman to resist the lure of a man's hairy armpits?

Many churches go to the extremes when it comes to modesty. No one should tell you what you should and should not wear. That is something between you and God.

THREE TYPES OF CLOTHING USUALLY DEEMED INAPPROPRIATE BY CHRISTIANS

(SORRY LADIES, TWO OF THE THREE HAVE TO DO WITH YOU.)

1   **Mini-skirt**—The mini-skirt comes in and out of style almost as often as Madonna. There is no set rule on how *short* is too short. But I will say this: Guys *like* to use our imagination—so let us!

2   **Bikinis**—I used to have a preacher who would ask the girls in the church if they would ever wear just their bra and panties out in public. I always thought that was a stupid question.

3   **Speedos**—Guys, I'm not sure there is EVER a good reason for us to wear a Speedo—I may let you slide if you're a swimmer. However, if you have ever worn a Speedo in public, no doubt your friends made fun of you behind your back. Hey, it's *your* ego, not mine.

PRE-MARITAL PHYSICAL CONTACT

When I was sixteen-years-old, my girlfriend and I were speeding down a dark back road; my left hand was steering my vintage 1983 blue Subaru GL, and my right hand was innocently resting on the emergency break located in the ten-inch space that separated Diane's seat from mine.

Suddenly I was overwhelmed by the most amazing sensation I had ever experienced in my life. It made me jump. I was so overcome with excitement that I almost lost control of the car. It was even better than eating my grandmother's homemade raspberry sorbet—half-melted—on a hot summer afternoon. It felt as though a-mind-numbing electricity was shooting from Diane's thumb and pointer finger, shocking through the tip of my middle finger to every one of my body's sensory organs. For the first time in my life, I was in physical contact with an attractive girl, and I wanted to scream.

Could it be that Diane wants to hold my hand? I thought. *I can't do this.*

My head was spinning in a thousand different directions. I tried to pull away, but I couldn't do it. It felt so good.

According to my church, I wasn't supposed to experience this kind of intimacy with a woman until I was married. What would

Diane's father do to me if he knew that right now my entire body was reacting in a fleshly way to the sweet touch of his daughter's left hand?

But I couldn't stop. It was as though my upper right appendage had a mind of its own. It longed to slide deeper into position. It wanted to know what it felt like to be inside Diane's hand.

Di's hand moved closer.

And once again that unbelievable feeling shot through every crevice of my body, leaving me with a helpless, "I-can't-turn-back-now" sense of lost control. I slid my hand inside hers. And our hands began to make the most passionate love that two virgin hands could possibly dream of. My fingers explored hers. Our hands moved in perfect rhythm. I was smirking on the inside because there was no doubt that I was good at this—*really* good.

FIVE TYPES OF "PHYSICALLY ACTIVE" COUPLES TO WATCH FOR IN CHRISTIAN CULTURE

1   **The closet hand-holders**—You know the couple I'm talking about. They're usually awkward, clumsy looking, and wear thick glasses. If you look for the couple who is "keeping each other warm" during church with a jacket blanketed over them, you'll no doubt catch them in the act! They're not cold; they're *really* holding hands.

2   **The baptistery make-out duo**—I'm not sure why, but every church with a in-house baptismal pool is always lucky enough to also get (free which the purchase) a young unmarried couple who frequents the baptistery for a quick one-on-one "dunking." This is just one more argument *against* immersion. Yikes.

3 **The youth-retreat hookup**—Every time my church would take us on a retreat, the youth pastor would discover a "new" couple taking a little retreat of their own in the back of the church van—WITH FIFTEEN OTHER PEOPLE IN THE VAN! What are these people thinking?

4 **The kiss-n-tell couple**—Oh, this couple always made me sick to my stomach. You know the type! They kiss each other and then they tell each other they can't continue dating because things got too heated up. Then they get back together. Then they kiss again. Then they break up—again. This cycle can continue for months.

5 **The fake-perfect couple**—She's a deacon's daughter. He's the pastor's son. They seemingly make the perfect couple. Everything seems so wonderful for them. They're the first couple to speak up against sex before marriage. They seem so pure, so righteous. They just seem … perfect! But then out of the blue, their world falls apart. You find out they have been having sex all along. Yet she's pregnant with his best friend's baby. The whole thing becomes this ugly church mess. They both have to leave the church. They never speak to each other again. And she ends up with a successful career talking to young girls about abstinence.

MASTURBATION

Like most college guys, my Christian college friends and I talked about sex a lot. My accountability group probably spent more time talking about sex and sex-related topics than anything else. In fact, I'm embarrassed to admit this, but the five guys in my weekly accountability group probably spent eighty percent of our time talking about sex. And at least seventy-five percent of *that* time was wasted discussing the very touchy topic of masturbation.

On one such morning during accountability group, my friend Joey decided it was time to once again open up about his struggles to the other four guys sitting around the circle. The five of us had just finished praying and reading our Bibles, and now it was time for open forum.

"Hey guys," Joey began bluntly, "I'm having a problem with masturbation again." Joey regularly struggled with masturbation. "I can't stop doing it," he insisted. "I think I'm addicted."

There's always one guy in every accountability group who is constantly struggling with some sin or spiritual issue. In my small group, that guy was Joey. But in reality, I think Joey was just more honest than the rest of us. We all struggled. We just didn't want to talk about it. Joey, however, had no scruples about sharing his problems. Every week we'd hear something new about Joey's secret past, such as his dirty thoughts, masturbation habits, girl troubles, or lack of God time.

"Guys," he continued anxiously, "I'm *whacking* off almost every day."

"Aw, come on, Joey!" Tim protested. "Stop! We don't want to hear anything else!" Tim was the quietest guy in our group, nervous and shy and self-righteous. He was studying to be a church choral leader—undoubtedly the wimpiest major our university had to offer. When Joey started sharing, it never took Tim long to get really uncomfortable.

But I shook my head at Tim in disgust.

"Joey," I said knowingly, "all of us struggle with masturbation." I looked around the circle at the other guys, expecting heads to nod in agreement. Except none of them were looking at me; they all just stared awkwardly into their closed Bibles.

"Thanks, guys, for leaving me hanging!" I cut off the embarrassed silence and turned to Joey. "Buddy," I continued, "I know what you mean. It's difficult not to masturbate. Don't think you're alone on this; we're just not as open about it."

"I've *never* masturbated," Geoff stated firmly. "Never!" Geoff, the tallest and best-looking of the group, was also the self-appointed spiritual leader. He would always try to bring the topic back around to God. But bringing a discussion back in from one of Joey's sexual tangents was usually way beyond even Geoff's leadership skills.

"You've *never* masturbated?" I said incredulously, in my best "you are completely full of crap" tone.

"No!" Geoff insisted.

It's not like I had proof that Geoff's hand had been in the cookie jar, but I had always heard that ninety-five percent of men have masturbated and the other five percent are lying. In Christian circles, however, it's not uncommon to meet a lot of guys who claim they have never pleasured themselves. In my small group, it was almost as though avoiding masturbation was some kind of spiritual thermometer. The more you forsook your body's desires, the more spiritual you were. This kind of thinking is ridiculous.

I recently interviewed a thirtysomething Christian speaker who claimed he hasn't masturbated in ten years—and he's *not* married. To be blatantly honest, I don't believe him. I told a youth pastor friend about this individual's astonishing feat and his comment to me was, "Gosh, I thought I was doing well going without it for a week after coming home from Thanksgiving vacation." We laughed.

Needless to say, no amount of discussion is ever going to get Christians to agree on issues of sexuality. Masturbation is simply one of those titillating topics from which churches may never find satisfying release.

FIVE FACTS ABOUT MASTURBATION
(DIRECTLY RELATED TO THINGS I WAS TAUGHT FROM MY CHURCH)

1 Taking cold showers and doing pushups do not relieve sexual tension.

2 The story in the Bible about Onan "spilling his seed" is not about masturbation.

3 Masturbation, as an act, is not mentioned in the Bible.

4 Masturbation does not cause warts or erectile dysfunction—*at least, it hasn't yet.*

5 The sudden guilty feeling that happens to guys after masturbation is a "physical" reaction, not spiritual.

THE CLIMAX

Sex has always been a funny, awkward topic for Christians to discuss. Yet despite it being difficult to talk about, it's very important that we become more willing to discuss sexuality—and more than just saying abstain from it! Regardless of what people say, feel, or are willing to admit, unmarried Christians are indeed having sex. In fact, there have been some studies that suggest sexual activity is as common among unmarried Christians as it is among non-Christian unmarried couples. And as long as Christian men and women pursue relationships, I don't see the battle for purity ending anytime soon—not because Christians are losing, but because the battle is not a flesh battle, it's of the heart. Jesus is quoted as saying in Mark 7: 21-23, "It is the thought-life that defiles you. For from within, out of a person's heart, come evil thoughts, sexual immorality, theft, murder, adultery, greed, wickedness, deceit, eagerness for lustful pleasure, envy, slander, pride, and foolishness. All these vile things come from within; they are what defile you and make you unacceptable to God."

CHRISTIAN
ENTERTAINMENT AND BOOKSTORES

CHRISTIAN ENTERTAINMENT AND BOOKSTORES
Chapter 9

I have been reviewing and critiquing Christian music and entertainment for years now. It's an enjoyable task, yet one that certainly is prone to giving me headaches and leaving me frustrated. Christians who make Jesus-oriented entertainment have been criticized not just by me, but also from other media facets, for creating sub par music, movies, and television. It's "stuff" that simply imitates what is popular and financially successful in the mainstream industry, but Christians usually (not always, but usually) do it badly. I have said many times that when it comes to entertainment and music, Christians seem to be at least two to five years behind the rest of the entertaining world. The areas where we lag behind are very important ones too. Yeah, creativity, production, finances, and profitability are pretty important facets to the success of any business.

Our substandard approach to entertaining the evangelical masses is not only belittling to Christians, it's hardly a good representation of our faith. Now, some have argued, "But look around, Matthew. You don't see Muslims and Buddhists creating *any* entertainment. At least Christians are doing something." And to that I reply: Other religions pour finances into mainstream music and movie making. Scientology has been said to be a huge contributor to Hollywood's pocketbooks. But to the contrary, Christians have created their own entertainment industry of sorts. We have our own

TV channels (TBN). We have our own record labels (Sparrow, Word, Reunion). We have our own movie companies (Cloud Ten Pictures). As a result, we have set ourselves up to not only compete with mainstream culture's entertainment industry, but we do it with the motives of preaching, making money, and bringing glory to God.

A COUPLE MESSAGES FOR CHRISTIAN MUSIC ARTISTS
(JUST IN CASE YOU FORGOT)

➡ Just because we're Christians does not mean we desire boring live shows where the artist pretends to be a rock star praising Jesus. We paid good money for an evening of entertainment, so bring on the fun!

➡ We love praise and worship music! And to be honest, we love to hear you say, "This night is all about God, and not this band." But please remember we weren't born yesterday. When you're prancing around the stage in tight leather pants, with a flashy light show making you look all sexy and cool, while singing "Open the Eyes Of My Heart"— we go home wondering why.

It's not necessarily a bad thing that we have created such a conglomerate of "Jesus" businesses. But now that we have this "industry," let's do a better job of creating excellent and compelling content that is both relevant and groundbreaking, and stop regurgitating "Christian" renderings of what already exists.

Unfortunately, the few times where Christian artists, musicians, and moviemakers have created pioneering content in recent years, either the gatekeepers in the Christian industry haven't accepted their art (Kendall Payne, Chasing Furies, Kevin Max) or we force the artist to go outside our industry to find another audience (P.O.D., Sixpence None The Richer). But unlike the few examples of success we have seen in the Christian music arena, attempts at Christian TV channels/shows and Christian movies haven't faired near as well. Which may be a good thing ...

REMEMBER THESE THINGS

FIVE WAYS TO MAKE YOURSELF A BETTER CHRISTIAN ENTERTAINER

1 **Remember your audience**—It seems recently that Christian entertainment has become more concerned about the bottom line than about what the audience's needs are.

2 **Remember your budget**—If you don't have the budget for really good special effects, then don't use special effects. Wow your audience some other way!

3 **Remember your story**—People connect with you because they relate to your story. That is your silver bullet! Don't ever forget that.

4   **Remember your reason**—Sometimes we have to take a moment and remember why we got into making entertainment in the first place. For your sake *and* for ours, please do this often.

5   **Remember your Creator**—God created you to be where you are! So for goodness sake, consult Him OFTEN on what you should do next. He will tell you.

MOVIES

Allow me to be blunt and say this: Christian movies are normally dreadful. Have you watched a Christian movie before? Take my advice: DON'T DO IT! *EVER!* Christian movies are like Lifetime movies, but worse. In fact, Lifetime movies might be Academy Award-worthy compared to the Christian movies I have seen. I don't believe I have ever seen a good one. I actually get embarrassed watching these flicks. I'm embarrassed for the people who spent the money to make the films. I get embarrassed for the male and female actors who seemingly lower themselves to the standards of faith-based cinema.

It isn't for the lack of creative ideas that Christian movies are bad. I think the problem may be bigger than that.

For instance, let's consider *Left Behind: The Movie*, which probably is the most successful Christian movie made in the last ten years. (Keep in mind this all changed with the release of Mel Gibson's *The Passion Of The Christ*, which grossed more than $300 million at the box office.)

FIVE MUST-DOS WHEN WATCHING A CHRISTIAN-MADE MOVIE

1 You MUST watch it with a close Christian friend. It makes the eighty-six minutes go much faster.

2 You MUST look past your tendency to have "I could have written a better script than this one" thoughts. Yes, you're right! You could have written a better script, but you didn't, did you?

3 You MUST have a strong drink (of course, I mean coffee) at your disposal to make the feeling of "Oh my Gosh, this is the worst movie ever" subside.

4 You MUST look past the poorly acted "action" scenes. Yes, that IS Kirk Cameron holding an everyday VCR camera with bombs going off in the background.

5 You MUST watch seventy-nine minutes of the movie in one sitting; the last seven minutes are always optional.

The concept of taking a mega-successful book and turning it into a movie is brilliant. Hollywood does it all the time. Gosh, John Grisham is a multi-millionaire due to Americans eating up his action-packed judicial drama time and time again. However, the Christian movie company Cloud Ten Pictures, which according to rumors is currently in pre-production for a television series called *Left Behind*, bought the rights to *Left Behind: The Movie* and spent a mere $20 million on the film. Twenty million dollars may sound like an incredible amount of money, but in Hollywood's terms, it's a drop in the bucket. And to be honest, I believe Cloud Ten could have made *Left Behind* a good movie without spending $100 million. But attempting to recreate special effects sequences without a budget is not the way to do it. And over and over again, Christian movie companies make an effort to get away with low-dollar special effects. As a substitute for spending the cash on effects that are put to shame by 1976's *Star Wars*, Christian movie companies with limited budgets should instead concentrate on gripping dialogue, compelling acting, and giving the audience a good story. Unfortunately, *Left Behind: The Movie*, a concept with good potential, received apocalyptic reviews and set Christian moviemaking back to the early-'80s.

The next big attempt to redeem Christian moviemaking will be when billionaire and Christian Phillip Anschutz, along with his company Walden Media, brings C.S. Lewis' *The Lion, The Witch and The Wardrobe* to the big screen in 2005. Rumor has it that the intended budget for the film is $170 million—which sounds pretty good.

TELEVISION

I'll never forget the first time I was flipping through my basic cable channels with the remote control and stopped on the well-known and quite popular Christian television channel, the Trinity Broadcasting Network.

My first thoughts? *Oh my gosh, there's a woman with big whitish, pink hair (looking to be a wig) and wearing fake eyelashes and bright, thick*

makeup on my television screen crying, praying, and preaching. Hey Mom!
Come here; you have to see this!

I'm not trying to be mean or insensitive, but someone please explain to me who watches this? Who wakes up in the morning and says to himself, "I'm going to pour me a cup of hot tea and sit down in front of the television and watch Jan Crouch for an hour"? This makes no sense to me. But apparently people do it.

One morning I decided to try it for myself. I made a warm cup of coffee and sat down for a fun-filled hour of Paul and Jan. She cried. He prayed. She cried some more; he prayed some more and then preached. This is compelling programming? Well, I have to admit, it was a lot better than anything on The UPN, but that's really not saying much.

FOUR IDEAS TO HELP TBN

1 **Lose the wig**—Big pink hair didn't even work for Cyndi Lauper—and she was cool!

2 **New musical talent**—You don't have to go to the musical extremes, but tone-savvy singers would be a welcomed blessing! Dried up Christian singers from the '80s are probably not the network's best options.

3 **Less crying and more compelling storytelling**—I want to hear more about what you're doing with all of

that money to help people around the world and less of
people weeping.

4   **Encourage, don't guilt us in to giving**—If your
ministry is useful, and the millions of people who are
influenced daily says that it is, then ask your audience
to partner with you and don't promise them earthly
reward—God NEVER promised us that. He said store up
treasures in heaven.

My father always taught me that if something is worth doing,
it's always worth doing right. I believe Christians still haven't
grasped this old saying. Eventually, we'll learn that when our faith is
publicly displayed poorly through art, music, books, movies, or TV,
or when preachers who are seemingly only interested in making
the next dollar glamorize the faith, all of us lose. Regrettably, when
everything the Christian culture puts out is supposedly done in the
name of Christ, culture doesn't differentiate between the good, the
bad, and the ugly—it's just collectively called Christian. And sadly, in
this case, that word doesn't mean Christ-like.

THE CHRISTIAN BOOKSTORE

Christian bookstores are a huge blessing. They certainly saved
my life, when I was a teenager.

I'll never forget the first time I stepped inside a Christian
bookstore. I was fifteen years old, and Mom and I were Christmas
shopping in a city about an hour away from my hometown. I had

heard rumors that stores like this existed, but I could hardly believe the stories I had heard. I couldn't wait to find out if they were true.

When I walked inside the store for the first time, I felt like I'd just entered the pearly gates. Music posters were hanging on the outside windows. A huge, beautiful picture of Amy Grant hung from the rafters of the ceiling. I had just walked smack-dab into a world I had never experienced, a place where Christianity was actually cool.

When I was able to overcome the first shock and look around at all the things for sale, I could hardly believe my eyes. I was standing in the middle of a ten-thousand square-foot building filled with every Christian item imaginable. There were incredibly cool Christian T-shirts, a huge Christian music section, Jesus pencils and pens, Jesus jewelry and magnets and crosses, Bible verse plaques, and Christian books on everything from speaking in tongues to Christ-like living. There was a whole shelf dedicated to just Christian fiction. The Lighthouse Christian Bookstore had everything I could ever want and more; it was like I had discovered the Christian Mecca, or at least Christianity's South of the Border.

WHAT WOULD JESUS DO WITH THAT?

FIVE CREATIVE IDEAS FOR YOUR OLD WWJD BRACELETS

1 They make great collars for small dogs and cats—even your ferret can get its Jesus-love on.

2 Turn your lust-a-lot Barbie into a bona fide believer with a WWJD "bracelet" headband or belt.

3 At the next wedding you attend, forget about throwing rice and birdseed or blowing bubbles—toss your WWJD bracelet at the newly christened husband and wife.

4 Hang your old bracelet on any doorknob. It's a great conversation piece.

5 If you have more than six old bracelets, put them all on your next bottle of Coca Cola—they'll keep your hand from getting wet!

I wandered the aisles, drooling over every item in the store. I thought the F.R.O.G. (Fully Reliant On God) mug, with its picture of a cartoon frog holding a Bible, was awesome. I gazed longingly at the "I Love Jesus" pencils. I wanted faith pins for my jean jacket. There were Bibles, Bible study booklets, and Christian videos. I even saw non-King James Version translations of the Bible—I had no idea that they even existed. I looked through every single Christian poster and finally talked my mom into buying me a very colorful one with all the names of God written on it in a hundred different fonts.

I laughed at all the different T-shirts in the store. There were shirts with "Jesus Christ" written in the Coca Cola and Pepsi Cola fonts. One shirt had the Budweiser insignia printed on it, but it read "Be Wiser" instead. It offended me, but I had to admit that it was clever. For every pop cultural tagline, brand name, or trademark the world had slapped on a T-shirt in 1988, the Lighthouse Christian Bookstore had a "Christianed-up" Jesus imposter T-shirt for the born-again believer to wear.

THREE "JESUS JUNK" ITEMS CHRISTIANS SHOULD HAVE NEVER MADE

1   **Test-a-mints**—Freshening your breath and witnessing to your neighbor at the same time is a little difficult with the Scripture verse dissolving in your mouth.

2   **Anything "Jabez" other than the book**—We're all about receiving the blessings, but we don't need a clock, a journal, a framed print, a Bible cover, and a pair of boxers to remind us of that.

3   **The "Fish Eating Darwin" car decal**—Everywhere you look, there's a tan mini-van with the "Jesus fish eating the Darwin thingy" pasted on its bum. Why did we lower ourselves to the standards of evolution?

CHAPTER 10

AWAKENING
YOUR CHRISTIAN LIFE

→ FIVE WAYS TO STAY AWAKE DURING SERMONS

→ FIVE TEACHINGS TO SURVIVE ON

→ FIVE WAYS TO REKINDLE YOUR RELATIONSHIP WITH GOD

AWAKENING YOUR CHRISTIAN LIFE

Chapter 10

One of hardest parts about living the Christian life is staying motivated. Of course, boredom is a problem all people face from time to time. But I think Christians get frustrated about their lives a little easier than most. I think it's because along with having to live with the everyday demands that the greater culture sends our way, we also have this whole other "Christian" culture that has even bigger demands. It gets hard sometimes to function like a Christ-loving individual when the rest of the world seems to be all up in your face.

FIVE EASY IDEAS TO REKINDLE YOUR RELATIONSHIP WITH GOD
(IN NO PARTICULAR ORDER)

➡ Take a retreat away from your everyday life. Even if it's one day where you spend time in prayer, worship, and meditation, you'll have a healthier perspective afterward.

➡ Go have lunch with a spiritual mentor. All of us know people who seem to have things together. But as you'll find out, they deal with the same stuff you do. Jesus uses others in our lives to help encourage and direct us.

➡ Go to your local Christian bookstore and splurge on a new daily devotional. Daily readings are always a great way to kick-start your day spiritually.

➡ Evaluate your priorities. A person with their basic life priorities out of whack always runs the risk of feeling overloaded and worn-out. Take a second glance at what you deem important and make changes to your daily routine.

➡ Spend a day serving a local charity or helping an individual in need. Many times, when we're feeling overwhelmed with life, serving others is a great way to give us a fresh perspective on our own lives. If you don't know of anyone in need (which is highly unlikely), ask your pastor or youth pastor for a list of good causes in your area!

Believe me, I have gotten frustrated and bored with my Christian experience. And to make my situation a little worse, most of my friends would say that I have a little problem with being A.D.D. I have to admit, it's true; I have a hard time staying interested in things—especially churchy things.

It's happened recently. Sitting in church a few Sundays ago, I felt boredom overwhelming me only a few minutes into the sermon. It was a regrettable turn of events, because the praise and worship music had been great. And the baby dedications were at least entertaining; babies are so darn cute when they have a large captive audience. Even the offering—despite not having anything to contribute—was more enjoyable than the first few minutes of the pastor's sermon. So I got up and left.

Now, before you start jumping to uncharitable conclusions, let me assure you that I really did try to find interest in that sermon. But an unbearable "will this ever end?" feeling started to well up uncontrollably inside of me, and only *six* minutes into the sermon! I tried to shoo away the thought. But it was that all-too-familiar feeling that begins right after the uncontrolled yawning has started and only moments before your head starts doing that nodding thing. And it's so difficult to work through a feeling like that when the point of contention is still right in front of me, preaching away. It's not as though I could just stand up and say, "Hey Pastor, how are you doing today? Do you think you could tell a joke or something to help me overcome my lack of interest in what you have to say? You're really boring me quite a bit." So what else could I do?

Besides, the pastor hadn't even gotten to the introductory prayer yet. And it wasn't like I was sitting in the front row. I was at least one, two, three, FOUR rows back in an auditorium of twenty rows. So practically half the church didn't even see me leave.

And of those who did watch me walk out the back door, I think some of them were actually jealous. No, really. Some of them were definitely watching me with undisguised envy. *They* wanted to be the person confidently strutting out of the service. Haven't all of us had moments sitting in church when we secretly wished we had a non-emergency ailment or a roast burning in the oven at home— just something that would warrant leaving church a half-hour early?

Let's be honest. When a movie is boring, we walk out. When a TV show is boring, we turn it off. When a book is slow, we close it. So why should church be any different?

FIVE NEVER-FAIL WAYS TO STAY AWAKE DURING ANY SERMON

1   **A little spit**—That's right! It's a little gross, but if you spit into your hands and rub it in to your eyes, you wake up every time! Plus, for all you guys with self-inflated egos, you'll also have an audience interested in watching your stupid shenanigans.

2   **Self-inflicted pain**—Pain wakes anyone up! My advice is to go easy on yourself at first. You'll be awake in no time by just pulling a couple of pieces of hair out of your arm.

3   **Laser finger**—Imagination is a must on this one! Just pretend that the end of your finger is a powerful laser, and then start cutting away. If you have a good imagination, you can pretend that you're cutting people's heads off, making chandeliers fall, and slicing microphone stands in half. It's a bit out there, but really a lot of fun.

4   **Makeshift games**—My favorite game to play during church is Tic Tac Toe or Rock, Paper, Scissors—just make sure you're not disturbing the people behind you. "I Spy With My Little Eyes" is fun too.

5   **Red Bull**—This stuff tastes horrible, but wakes you up every time! Caffeine has always been the Christian's ultimate drug of choice!

PERSONAL AWAKENING

First impressions always amaze me. Sometimes you have no idea when you meet someone that this person is destined to powerfully impact your life forever.

When I first met James Langeaux, he had already changed my life. His book *God.com* had given me an unprecedented desire to really understand the attributes of God and how they relate to me. James and I had spoken on the phone many times, but we had never met in person. So when I attended a Christian music festival near James' California home one spring, I didn't hesitate to ask James if he would meet me for breakfast.

James is a short, thirtysomething, muscular, eccentric man with bleached-blond hair and piercing blue eyes. He pulled into the hippie-village coffeehouse where he had chosen to meet me in an ostentatiously noisy jeep, strutting up the sidewalk in his cut-off shorts and movie-star sunglasses like he owned the place. I was more than a little intimidated. *Oh my gosh*, I thought, *Who is this guy?*

Over sweet blueberry pancakes and strong black coffee, I tried to figure out the answer to that question. James was the most outlandish Jesus-lover I had ever encountered. He talked about Christ with the passion and enthusiasm that most people reserve for sex or money or football. He talked about Christ like it was sinful.

"Most Christians don't really believe, Matthew," James told me, his intense eyes boring into me. "They've joined a club. But when we join a club, we have no power. We're just members of a system that has some rules that make us feel comfortable. We really don't believe."

James was full of stories about true belief. He had traveled all over the world, following the promptings of a mysterious one-on-one conversation with God. His adventures included face-to-face encounters with miracles in Thailand, fanatical worship experiences in New Zealand, and beer-guzzling God-moments in Budapest. I wasn't sure I believed every story James told me. But I was amazed by this man's freedom, and I walked away from that breakfast conversation determined to take my own journey into the freedom of Christ.

THE TEACHINGS OF CHRIST

FIVE TEACHINGS OF CHRIST TO SURVIVE ON

1   Do not judge.

2   Love your neighbor, but more importantly, love your enemy.

3   Hunger and thirst after righteousness.

4   Love the Lord with all your heart, soul, mind, and strength.

5   Believe. Believe. Believe. Believe what He teaches with all of your heart.

I came home with James' words still ringing in my ears. "I have been powerless for a very long time," he had told me. "I've gotten into a lot of trouble while saying that I believed, and inside I'm still wrestling. But power comes when I really tap into believing and laying myself at Jesus' feet, admitting that I am a screwed-up mess and only Jesus can bring about a resurrection." The words that stuck with me the most was the verse that James had quoted to me. I could still see James' intense face as he said it: "He who the Son sets free, He is free indeed." That face was to me a picture of freedom—a freedom I had never even glimpsed in my own life.

LIVING OUT
YOUR FAITH

→ SEVEN EVANGELISM DON'TS

→ COMMON "CHRISTIAN" MISCONCEPTIONS

→ FIVE TRUTHS I LEARNED

LIVING OUT YOUR FAITH

Conclusion

Okay, so you've come to the last chapter! I hope your brain isn't overloaded with too much Christian culture babble. We've discussed a lot so far. From meeting Jesus for the first time to a Christian single's lack of a sex life, we've nearly covered the gamut of Christian culture topics—certainly not everything—but a lot. Well, this last chapter is about another very important topic: living out your faith. Living out your faith is probably the most important aspect of following Jesus. Although, like most things in Christian culture, there are many misconstrued ideas about "living out" Christ's love in culture.

Lately I've been watching a lot of *I Love Lucy* reruns on TV Land. One of my favorite episodes shows Lucy getting lost in Brooklyn with a "loving cup" stuck on her head. Unable to see, Lucy is desperately searching for someone to help her. A police officer looks at her situation and inquires politely, "Ma'am, would a police officer be of any assistance to you?" Not knowing who she's talking to, Lucy responds, "No, no, no. Don't get a policeman involved. You know how they're always getting into everybody's business and asking those nosey questions. The last thing I need is a police officer." Of course, the laugh comes when Lucy discovers that she is in fact speaking to a police officer. But I think Christians can learn something here. Sadly, society today tends to view Christians the same way Lucy viewed the police officer. Many times, Christians are seen as part of the problem and not part of the solution.

SEVEN EVANGELISM DON'TS

1 Do NOT leave a Jesus tract for a server in place of his or her eighteen percent tip. Gospel presentation pamphlets with less than fifteen percent tips don't work either!

2 Do NOT perform "quickie" salvation pitches on the streets of foreign cities. It's bad enough we do these in English on the streets of American cities, but give the rest of the world a break and at least have the decency to get to know the person first.

3 Do NOT be a participant in drive-by "evangelizements." I'm not sure anyone has ever come to salvation by hearing people yell Jesus messages from passing cars.

4 Do NOT witness while intoxicated, high, or after having unmarried sex. Oh! You would be shocked to know the stories I have heard.

5 Do NOT go into chat rooms and bash people because of their beliefs or lifestyle, and then try to tell them about Jesus. That rarely works!

6 Do NOT make wagers or bets regarding people's souls; salvation is never a game.

7 Do NOT underestimate the influence your life can have on an individual who doesn't know Jesus.

Sadly, most Christian denominations have spent the last 2,000 years trying to define Jesus in human terms, attempting to compress His teachings into supposedly more digestible tidbits. But we were never meant to *digest* the teachings of Jesus; we were meant to live them out. Today, we have such a limited understanding of how truly radical Jesus is. We're relying too heavily on our Christian books, Christian music, and TV evangelists to guide our thinking. We wear our silly Jesus T-shirts and jewelry and hang our Bible verse plaques, and we think we're proclaiming the name of Christ. We go to festivals, revivals, and church functions and call it true fellowship. We put "Jesus Saves" on a billboard and think we've done something really miraculous. We sing a few praise songs and listen to a man or a woman lecture on scripture, and we think we've experienced worship. We stand outside a courthouse and picket the removal of The Ten Commandments and think we're fighting the good fight. We hold up our signs reading "God Hates Fags" and truly believe we are helping to awaken a perverted culture. We join the "Christian" club and separate ourselves from the world, and the world still sits on the outside, dying for someone to demonstrate what it means to believe.

COMMON "CHRISTIAN" MISCONCEPTIONS ...
(A FEW THINGS TO THINK ABOUT)

➡ Just because you're wearing a Dr. Pepper-font "Jesus" T-shirt while sipping virgin daiquiris on the sand in West Palm Beach, doesn't mean you're being like the apostle Paul and advancing the kingdom.

→ Just because you're carrying around Rick Warren's *The Purpose Driven Life*, doesn't necessarily mean the force is with you.

→ Just because you're a writer for *USA Today*, an actor in an upcoming Jim Carrey movie, or a singer who is opening up for Joan Osborne, doesn't mean you're a "roaring lamb."

→ Just because your hands are lifted, your eyes are closed, and you're singing the latest praise song, doesn't mean you're worshiping.

→ Just because you love Jesus, doesn't make you a Republican.

About two years ago, sitting in a smoke-filled sports bar, I met Devon, a twenty-four-year-old gay white man trying his hardest to forget life's sorrows by downing his fourth apple martini. It obviously wasn't working, because he was sharing his entire life story with me, a stranger with a Jesus agenda.

I listened to Devon carefully, interjecting a question or two between his thoughts. Devon claimed to be a very moral gay man. I smiled ironically at the incongruity.

"I don't sleep around," he told me. "I haven't had sex in six months." He shook his head and took another sip of martini. "But I'm still a screwed-up mess."

He went on to tell me about his battle with depression that he said was caused by having been sexually abused by his uncle when he was ten years old.

"I had a f------ up childhood. I grew up Mormon, and now I'm gay; how's that for a combination?" he added with a wry grimace, absently drawing patterns on the bar counter with his finger.

"Do your parents know you're gay?" I asked gently.

"Nah," Devon shook his head emphatically. "They'd never understand."

"Why not?"

"Because the d--- Mormon Church condemns people like me," he retorted, looking up at me with fuzzy alcohol anxiety. His eyes narrowed as he peered at me. "Do you know anything about the Mormon Church?"

"A little," I said slowly. In all honesty, I actually thought I knew quite a bit, but the evangelical in me was on the prowl for a spiritual in. And I thought my chances for getting us on the "Roman's Road" would be better if I played it dumb.

"My parents just wouldn't understand." Devon said with finality. "At least, not right now."

"How do you think God feels?" I asked.

"Oh," he laughed, "God and I are fine. I pray to God. He talks to me."

"Really?" This time, I was honestly intrigued. "What does God say to you?"

"I know one thing; I'm pretty darn sure God doesn't care who I share a bed with."

"How do you know He doesn't care? He cares who I share a bed with. Why wouldn't he care about what you do?"

Devon smiled, shrugged off my comment, and took a drag of his cigarette.

I tried a different tactic. "Do Mormons believe in Jesus?" I asked him.

"Oh yeah, they do!" A slow smile spread across Devon's face. "I *love* Jesus," he assured me. "I have crucifixes all over my living room."

"You do? Why is that?"

"I think Jesus is sexy," he gloated, downing the last drop of his martini with a flourish.

I was shocked. "You think Jesus is what?" I gasped.

He ignored my question and lit up another Marlboro Light. "So what's your story?" he asked shortly, adding breezily with a nod at his cigarette, "I only social smoke."

"My story?" I wondered aloud, not sure I exactly knew what he was getting at.

"Are you religious?"

I thought about going right into the plan of salvation, but I thought it best to opt for a more subtle approach.

"I'm a follower of Jesus." I said carefully. "I go to the Presbyterian Church on 5th and Broadway. I love …"

"You know?" he interrupted, as excited as if he had just received an epiphany from heaven. "I don't go to church anymore. I have my own religion."

"Your own religion?" I said curiously.

"Well," he amended, "it's not exactly a religion. I just don't think I need a building and bad music to talk to God. I just try to be a good person."

I frowned. I had definitely been taught the Christian answer to that. "Do you think you're good enough?" I asked him, trying to laugh a little for subtle effect.

"Hell no, but I think God understands."

"Yeah, well," I interjected, feeling the conversation moving back toward my plan-of-salvation agenda, "I'm *sure* that *I'm* not good enough. But that's why Jesus …"

I was interrupted again—this time by Devon's flamboyant friend Johnny motioning to us that he was ready to leave.

"He's my ride," Devon said rolling his eyes. "I guess I had better go. It was really nice chatting with you."

Huh. You'd think that if God really wanted me to share the Gospel with this guy, He'd have slowed Johnny's impatience down at least until I finished my sentence. "You too," I said helplessly.

I watched Devon as he left the bar and went home that night feeling perplexed. I had tried to say the right things, but I knew I hadn't said anything life changing. Where was my ability to relate Christ to his situation?

I've learned the hard way that sharing a freeing Christ with others is so much more than saying good things and asking a few leading questions. It's passionately living the life that Christ taught us. It's walking in His footsteps. It's loving people unconditionally—even our enemies. It's believing the words Jesus spoke to us and then actually doing them. It's being confident in the love of Jesus and walking freely in His love. Unconditional love is something we rarely comprehend, but when it's acted out in life's everyday situations, the miraculous Gospel of Christ is preached. And the words we speak through actions are never in vain—although the words our mouths speak often go unheard. In other words, love the heck out of the people who cross your path—leave the rest to God.

It's an understatement for me to say I will never again allow Christian culture to define my relationship with Christ. I've learned that "This little light of mine, I'm gonna let it shine" doesn't mean wear T-shirts and jewelry, preach hellfire and brimstone, or pretend to be holy and blameless—it means letting the love, mercy, and freedom Christ demonstrated resonate through us. Although, I do recommend you take your Jesus T-shirts and hide them under a bushel. NO? Okay, never mind—maybe that's just me.

DESPITE WHAT YOU'VE HEARD

FIVE TRUTHS I HAVE LEARNED ABOUT LIVING OUT MY FAITH

1 Love never has an agenda—*never.*

2 I am always on call to be a missionary—even at three o'clock in the morning when I'm half asleep.

3 Despite what you've been told, Jesus loves lesbians, murderers, *and* legalistic fundamentalists.

4 Sometimes the most blatant, obnoxious witness for Jesus comes from the quietest person in the room.

5 No fear.

Get a FREE ISSUE of
RELEVANT magazine!

God. life. progressive culture.

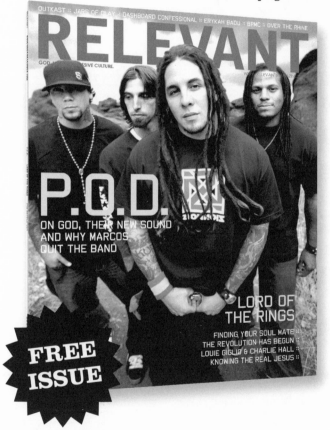

GET YOUR FREE ISSUE AT
www.RELEVANTmagazine.com/FreeIssue

—